Social Risks of Current Regulations

KINGA PÉTERVÁRI

Social Risks of Current Regulations

KINGA PÉTERVÁRI

L'Harmattan

L'Harmattan Kiadó
Kossuth Lajos utca 14–16.
H-1053 Budapest, Hungary

L'Harmattan France
5-7 rue de l'Ecole Polytechnique
75005 Paris

ISBN 978-2-343-25168-4

Volumes may be ordered, at a discount, from
L'Harmattan Könyvesbolt
1053 Budapest, Kossuth L. u. 14–16.
Tel.: +36-1-267-5979
harmattan@harmattan.hu

www.amazon.fr

CONTENTS

CHAPTER 2.
RISKS OF NON-DEVIATION FROM THE ABSOLUTE PRIORITY RULE IN BANKRUPTCY CASES 90

CHAPTER 3.
RISKS OF LEGAL ELITES IN LEGISLATIVE DRAFTING 104

INTRODUCTION

> *"Imagine that the keeper of a huge, strong beast notices what makes it angry, what it desires, how it has to be approached and handled, the circumstances and the conditions under which it becomes particularly fierce or calm…gently or wild… He calls it knowledge, forms it into a systematic branch of expertise, and starts to teach it, despite total ignorance, in fact, about which of the creature's attitudes and desires is commendable or deplorable, good or bad, moral or immoral… since he hasn't realised and can't explain to anyone else how vast a gulf there is between necessity and goodness."*
>
> (Plato: The Republic 493a-c)

This book is about *risk assessment, risk analysis* and *risk management* from a legal point of view. It discusses five different types of risks that business law needs to cope with nowadays. Some of these challenges are fairly new (artificial intelligence, AI), some are fairly old (limited liability), but they all trigger serious social challenges.

The risks are *global* in nature and independent from the existence of the state. Law, however, – as we know it so far – is local and particular, entirely dependent on the existence of the state. These challenges therefore are to be dealt with *interdisciplinary methods*.

The risks provoked by the old challenges and the new changes are also *definitively universal* as opposed to the legal issues which, despite all developments, are still case-dependent. This perception does not claim that the law is incapable of handling changes. It only demonstrates that the law is always case-specific: someone wins at the court, hence the other one loses, someone wins at the election hence other ones lose. Some problems are universal, some are global but none can be managed by the locally defined law. The controversy at hand will be decided, but the problem would not even be touched. Universal problems are not necessarily global: e.g. the right for housing or the fact that most people live in cities. But even these issues require interdisciplinary approaches. Because the law still remains local and particular. Law, by definition, belongs to the realm and the existence of statehood, thus, the efficiency, the possibilities and the means of the law are predetermined by this relationship. No law exists without the state and the specific nature of the state specifies the actual law and its enforcement.

The examined phenomenon here is the "risk" itself, as well as how to assess, analyze and manage it by and beyond the toolkit of the law. Risks cannot be tackled locally, since businesses (firms and entrepreneurs) would leave the country right away if they felt threatened by restrictions imposed by the law. And businesses can do that legally in free trade areas, or in customs unions. The EU law is just the treasure trove of this sort of problems: free riding and forum-shopping. Environmental problems, limited liability issues or workers' rights cannot be handled simply with taxation or specific particular laws if the market participants (firms, entrepreneurs, states) do not cooperate, do not observe the agreements. Law is attributed with an inborn double characteristic. It can be understood either as a norm or as an operation. If law is interpreted in its role as a norm, then its imperious element is enforceability, as opposed to other kind of norms, like moral or religious. The ultimate authority, the power of the state to enforce a court decision is inevitable for the law to be efficient. If, however, law is considered to be a procedure, as a tool or method for operating things, then enforceability is not a prerequisite for its concept. Participants or actors of the field may cooperate with each other, may agree on their own terms to follow. Instead of going to court, the parties may accept to pay for their choices. Or, instead of claiming a right for due public services, one may choose to pay for it in the private sector – like many citizens do it in order to avoid waiting lists or shortages in the public health care system in Hungary. This kind of *preater iuram* means may also be a good starting point for risk management.

But most importantly, risks, and not only the seldom occurrent ones, can be extremely high, and the damages can be overwhelming. *When these risks come about, it does not matter who is right and who is not.*

These challenges of the regulations are presented through *five different types of risks* in this book. *Part 1.* is about the *new risks materialized by artificial intelligence and the internet* (web2.0 at least). Until the appearance of AI, the evolution of things could be described with the means of the law, mainly by using analogy. At the beginning one could perhaps say that the robots are „like" slaves or animals, promptly triggering various responses from philosophers, neurologists and psychologists alongside the sociologists or economists addressing free will, others' minds, power and poverty. Questions arose like how many bugs are to be acceptable in a software in case of a car crash? Who should be liable for an autonomous vehicle when it follows the rule and when it does not? How to tame the regulation by design to be more like a rule of law?

In the epoque of web2.0, charactetized by machine learning and the application of big data, however, the classic legal examination seems to be insufficient. The risks and the possible damages are often unforeseeable, thus the compensation for the damages in case of objective liability (strict liability) is capped. Also, with the web2.0 traditional legal institutions become blurred. For example, there are no clear owners in case of the content-providing.

Also, internet connects two parallel but intertwined worlds: the on-line and the off-line. If softwares are defect on the internet it has physical consequences in the real world. With its connecting nature, internet inserts a third assisting party into all on-line transactions. The role of the traditional actors is blurry and extra risks are to be dealt with. The risks of competence and liability, thus create novel challenges.

Part 2. discusses the *social risks and external costs of the regulations.* In Chapter 1. these risks are related to the *layman's legal consciousness.* The risk emerges with the problem that the legal consciousness of the private persons, indebted or not, do not match the requirements of long-settled rules and regulations, i.e. contractual promises. Although legal consciousness is clearly concurrent in primary material cases, it is not the case when the question is about repayment of the loan agreements. It means that the laws on murder or theft are not divergent from what people would think about them generally and specifically. This contradiction triggers and frames the case study of a possible interpretation of current Hungarian *financial-legal culture,* focusing on how to apply those terms and conditions in long-term loan agreements in financial crisis, which are favorable or seemingly irrelevant in good times but turn out to be disadvantageous, sometimes even disastrous in bad times. This discrepancy between perception and regulation is a clear risk. Questions discussed here include how to calculate and allocate risks, what is acceptable and what is foreseeable to laymen? The focus here is on the laymen's attitudes towards long-term contractual obligations and performances in the global financial crisis, including whether debtors' contractual obligations must be fulfilled, or what should be construed as an excuse for non-performance, and whether there should be measures designed to protect the debtors more? Also, if the answer is affirmative, then at whose expense – the creditors (through preventive measures) or the taxpayers (through restitutive measures). If the answer is no, then how should we allocate ideally the risks and liabilities? And in general: is profit-making an evil *per se,* that needs to be managed?

Chapter 2. is a reflection on a case study screening the bankruptcy rules and the actual bankruptcies among the Hungarian SMEs. Here *the risks address the classic sociological problem of doubling personalities.* Whereas limited liabilities enable private persons to multiply their capital, yet they remain insulated from direct coverage of their (their firm's) debts, unless they scienter cause damages to the company or the creditors. This kind of possibility erases the need for the old-fashioned suicide in case of hopeless debts. Nevertheless, insolvent companies need to be tackled somehow, often globally. Thus, risk management with limited liability is a safety net for private persons (and a source of the capital), yet these insolvencies are a burden on other stakeholders (creating free riding problems).

Further elements of these risks include the globalization of debts and limited liabilities. Bankruptcies carry important information for the market which becomes even more relevant since insolvency is often not caused by the company's failure or inefficiency, but by external impacts like chain debts. The goal of the competition rules in these cases is to ensure the return of the expectations developed by the interested parties – debtors and creditors – at the time of investment. This is the way to protect the trust of the participants in the financial markets and in the businesses, and thus compensate for the risks.

Chapter 3. addresses the *risks generated by the legal elite*. As a rule of thumb, the academic elite is evidently an 'elite' only in the context of the academia, in the field of their expertise, and not in every aspect of life or profession. Although researchers describe the methods and narrate the operation of various institutions, no one would believe that they could perform equally well in practice. *Vice versa*, just like businesses are carried out in the market of competing companies and the CEOs, CFOs and other managers would not be equally successful in the market of academics. Economists teaching at universities usually do not vindicate that they know how to make money as CEOs: if this was the case, they would be doing it instead of teaching. In the legal field however, this distinction is blurred. Law professors not only teach the rules but also make it. Thus, uniquely for lawyers, law professors also claim to have a competence of law-making, and legislative drafting. If this was the case in the realm of the business, academics would be CEOs of big businesses and would steer the companies. It is more likely than not that legal academics are the best performing, best self-interest-promoting legal professional group, because they have the opportunity to disguise their interests by pretending their social identity as representatives of objectivity, using scientific methodology, and legal rationality.

PART 1.

NEW RISKS OF NEW TECHNOLOGIES

CHAPTER 1.

RISKS OF REGULATING AUTONOMOUS VEHICLES[1]

The first chapter is about autonomous vehicles and the adjacent legal problems. Whether this challenge, however, adds up to a paradigm shift in legal thinking is to be seen and analyzed further. As robotics develop globally, legal institutions need to keep pace with it, because business risk, such as liability, has to be reasonably calculable for investors. Due to the expansive applicability of robotics, the legal questions are manifold. The law faces applicatory as well as regulatory challenges. What is the standard for an autonomous vehicle? What should be the safety standards in driverless cars? How many bugs are to be acceptable in a software in case of a car crash? Who should be liable for an autonomous vehicle when it follows the rule and when it does not? How to tame the regulation by design to be more like a rule of law? This chapter focuses on pragmatic problems and solutions and new regulatory models, like regulation by communication. It also introduces the concept of stealthy technologies, the meaning of which is that no matter what the rule is innovative technologies are going to be overwhelmingly widespread.

1. Introduction

Since there is no consensual opinion on what the paradigm as such means in social sciences, including legal sciences, this chapter does not serve with a direct answer to the question whether or not there is a paradigm shift in legal thinking. Yet, one thing is certain. There are many changes in our contemporary, specific world which could generate the feeling of radical difference. But do they touch upon basic legal principles too? The real debatable question is then whether profound changes or whether many profound changes, would cause paradigm shift. The exact answers will undoubtedly be delivered by the numerous decisions of the legislation and the law enforcement in the near future.

Having said that, however, in this chapter it is going to be shown that the law, as it is today, operates with analogies and fictions. And as long as there are analogies and precedents or fictions available, one is not crossing the border of normal sciences, the territory of one paradigm. Obviously, there are, and has never been homologous cases, legislators and/or judges always apply the interpretations of the previous cases.

[1] For an earlier version of this chapter, see: K Pétervári and K Pázmándi 2018 IOP Conf. Ser.: Mater. Sci. Eng. 448 012030: Law and Economic Analysis of the Legal Environment Related to the Autonomous Vehicles – Is There a Legal Paradigm Shift?

The chapter here, therefore, relies on the use of analogies too. It analyses the various legal tools applicable to the relevant cases, such as the legal personality, the vicarious liability and the culpability as opposed to strict – objective – liability. Again, one thing is certain. All of these legal techniques were familiar in the course of the legal history, none of these are new, but perhaps their applicability of scale is different. Since law is a social construction, the conceptions of the various legal tools may change. But even the most radical recommendation of awarding a computer a legal personality, or constitutional fundamental rights, can found its roots in the past, like legal personality to organs created by the law, such as the companies, or the standing for the trees, which provides now legal protection to the environment.

On the other hand, one might object, that the new suggested models of regulation could cause a paradigm shift in legal thinking. These are the regulation by design or the regulation by communications. Regulation designers, like system designers, software engineers, and so on, need to find out the language what computers speak, and be able to speak the same language, also with the lawmakers and courts and the law enforcement people.

Yet, this chapter would introduce a new conception: the stealthy automatics or stealthy technology. With this term this chapter argues, that whatever the regulation may be the autonomous cars are going to ameliorate and widespread.

2. The regulatory challenge

2.1. Analogies in regulating: EU v. USA

Unlike the other rivalling companies back in 2016, Uber, this innovative but fairly eccentric company, refused to apply for a permit in San Francisco when launched a test driving of its autonomous vehicles (Wired (2016/12). Although the new rules of California would have so required, and the authorities so enforced indeed, Uber deliberately chose to remain under the scope of the old regulations. Truly, the cars on the streets are driverless, but there is always an engineer behind the wheels, ready to intervene and so autonomous vehicles qualify as vehicles driven in a "conventional mode", Uber argued.

Unlike California, however, Pittsburgh, Pennsylvania, where Uber had its basic testing sites, did not have new rules on autonomous vehicles operating in the city. Since then Uber has launched there its taxi services with a driverless car fleet. Lyft followed suit quickly (Wired 2016/12).

The rivalry among manufacturing companies of autonomous vehicles is recently so tense, that one must but wonder, whether the rules matter at all. These cases do not mean that there are no regulations whatsoever, though. Interestingly enough, one of the first statements of the US federal authorities asserted the continuity of the existing structure of the legal institutions, namely that "the division of regulatory responsibility for motor vehicle operation between Federal and State authorities is clear... should remain largely unchanged for highly autonomous vehicles" (NHTSA Policy Guidance, 2016).

The Europeans in the EU have somewhat analogous experiences but with a philosophically different attitude. Whereas it is a federal competence in the USA to decide who can access the public roads, this decision belongs rather to the competence of the Member States in the EU, so far, at least. And the Member States do use their power to regulate, and they regulate fairly disparately, of course. The Hungarian version of modification, for example, deals merely with the testing of the highly automated vehicles (11/2017. (IV. 12.) NFM order), whereas the German one applies to the traffic itself, even if under strict scrutiny (Achtes Gesetz zur Anderung des Strassenverkehrsgesetzes, vom 16. Juni, 2017). In any event, due to its determinant effect on the internal market, the EU will have to act at Union level.

The EU has, however, a rather ambiguous approach to the matter. It has shared competence in transportation policy (Article 4.2.(g) TFEU), but transportation in its stricter sense. It means that as far as it is indispensable for the common trade policy or competition within the internal market, this area is covered by the competence of the EU. So the EU legislators are abide by the otherwise classical notion of subsidiarity principle and proportionality principle. Under the principle of subsidiarity, "in areas which do not fall within its exclusive competence, the Union shall act only if and insofar as the objectives of the proposed action cannot be sufficiently achieved by the Member States,... but can rather, by reason of the scale or effects of the proposed action, be better achieved at Union level" (Article 5.3 TFEU). Further, the proportionality principle compels that the EU "shall not exceed what is necessary to achieve the objectives of the Treaties" (Article 5.4 TFEU).

On the other hand road safety does not only extend to the commercial attributes of transportation, but also to the very basic idea of the European integration. Therefore one might argue that free movement requirements trigger broader EU competences. Besides, the EU has again another kind of competence to act, namely "to carry out actions to support, coordinate or supplement the actions of the Member States in certain areas such as (a) the protection and improvement of human health; (b) industry or (d) tourism" (Article 6 TFEU), which all involve the very issue of the autonomous vehicles too.

These complicate structures of the EU, actually boil down to various, often soft, legal tools regarding road safety and autonomous vehicles, like declarations (Valletta Declaration on Road Safety, 2017), resolutions (Motion of the European Parliament (2015/2103(INL), guidelines but also directives (framework directive 2007/46/EC on type-approval of motor vehicles) and regulations (Regulation (EU) 2017/1154 on type-approval of motor vehicles). This structure of the legal competence in Europe is, therefore, conspicuously more complex, than that of the USA. Especially because the relevant authorities of the Member States still have further room for manoeuvre to regulate, since it is not yet preempted by the EU.

Yet, it is not preempted in the USA either. The U.S. Code, Title 49, Chapter 301-305 on motor vehicle safety, standards and compliances, which basically corresponds to the EU regulations on type-approval of motor vehicles, is not yet adjusted to the automated vehicles, therefore many states issued special regulations. Having wished to stop that regulatory wave of the States, the Obama Administration in 2016 allowed the federal supervisory regulating agency (NHTSA) to preliminarily exempt some automated vehicles from the compulsory compliance with certain requirements, until the Department of Transportation, DOT, elabourated an acceptable version of new regulations. This exemption seems to be approved in both actually, competingly, debated Senate and House Bills and even in a growing scale (Senate Bill: S.1885, House Bill HR 3388). Thus in 2020 there would be 100.000 such driverless cars in the public roads in the USA. The justification seems to be that technology becomes ever better and the driverless cars are much safer than the conventionally driven cars are.

In addition to the tiring issue of division of competences related to the topic, there are, however, other differences between the US and EU regulations: firstly the divergent structure of the EU and the USA, secondly the divergent way of approach to the regulation as such and thirdly, the divergent basic legal institutions applicable in this field.

Certainly, due to its lacking of federalism, the cross-border incidents in the EU can trigger international law further complicating the legal problems, like in the case of a cross-border accident (Kiilunen 2018, Pétervári 2017, Nagy 2010). Mostly for this reason, the EU also employs a more administrative approach towards regulation, since it lacks the real power of enforcement, so the ticking of the check box in the compliance procedures is rather convenient. But this might not serve the interest of the competing industry. The recent regulatory approach of the USA has, on the other hand, been very much innovative and competition-friendly above all. The exemption policy puts the risk of bad regulation, or no regulation whatsoever, on the federal regulatory agency. In the meantime not even the States may legislate on the safety requirements of a driverless car, albeit especially big cities are tempted.

Needless to point out, that the mainstream European approach is conceptually different. Already at the beginning of the 2010's various working groups in the EU suggested a "top to the bottom" approach to the legal problems of robotics (Leroux – Labruto, 2012 10). Certainly, there are rather convincing arguments supporting this attitude, like avoiding wastes by not investing in competing but failing research projects and thereby gaining time. Nevertheless there is no guarantee, that an action plan based on administrative prescriptions, no matter how deliberated it is, will serve a safer and quicker result. All such an approach can assure is, that whatever the result is, it will be expensive. This undoubtedly provides less smooth pathway for innovative manufacturers, since the burden of risk will be held by the industry and not the administration. Surely, however this burden of risk will ultimately be paid by the consumers, and the risk in this kind of world of innovation is generally allocated to the tax-payers. This may not be unfair but less efficient.

Not surprisingly, though, in certain fields, the stakeholders may dictate in both worlds. The driverless cars run first of all in cities all over the world and both the US and the EU concentrate the scope of regulations on automated vehicles to the lighter type of cars. Thus, for example, lorries cannot be exempted in the USA. This may seem to be counterfactual, though, since automated lorries are expected to be less dangerous rolling on the public roads (like OTTO of Uber) than the automated cars in the cities. Nevertheless due to the existing fear of employees, and the governments, the stakeholders' concerns are very strong and seemingly deserved legislative attention in this and other primarily robotics threatened industries.

The lack of the necessary skills to understand the applied technology makes the law-makers and the courts vulnerable to this controversial information asymmetry and might also have a disadvantageous impact on applying less reasoning and more technical slang. The unintended acceleration problems in car crashes in the Toyota case of 2009 are good examples to that. The jury may not be competent enough to decide on real causation, some experts claim. Whether the undeniably many bugs in a software can be proven to directly lead to fatal crashes, that is the question. In traffic accidents the driver's negligence needs to be shown to find him liable under common law. The driver can defend himself by claiming, that it was not his fault but that of the car. Then the so called proximate cause has to be evidenced, namely, that the accident is the direct causation of the existence of all those bugs in the cars' software. And then the real question is, if an expert witness explains to the jury that the standard of the numbers of the bugs allowed in "one software": is zero, or maximum 5-6, and in the "relevant software" there are 1000 of them, then if the jury can count, the software producer will definitely be found liable, no matter whether that is verified to calculate the bugs so (Cummings 2017, Parrish 2016). Although in this case Toyota finally lost generating billions of dollar damages, these sort of product liability situations do not necessarily end so. And what is more, especially in the case of driverless cars there is no "one software" or it is almost impossible to track down the "relevant software", let alone the possibility of the car to develop "own softwares" with the deep learning method.

The new challenges provoke new models and there are various possible answers for how to create an architecture of the regulation by design and how to make designers be responsible for it. Some argue for translation from the real space to the cyberspace (Lessig 1999), a commitment to moral understandings and values in technical regulations too (Urquhart – Rodden 2016), application of the rule of law considerations in the cyberspace too (Murray 2013) or language gaming, design by communications (Koops – Hildebrandt – Jaquet-Chiffelle 2010). These are all important issues so that to ascertain on whom to allocate the risk, the burden of proof, the impossibility of proving or the impossibility of foreseeability, to name but a few.

2.2. The regulatory challenge - are there robot-subjects or do the robots have legal personhoods/personalities

In fact, the regulatory challenge, related to the automated vehicles, is that it encompasses obviously many more legislative areas than just that of the transportation. Safety on roads covers a lot more than just a physical well-being or simply a being on the roads without accident.

Driverless cars create new environment. It presumes swiftly communicating softwares of others and complex infrastructures. But, most importantly, it allows on the spot decision-making without human interference. Apart from the usual technological development problems, therefore, this all requires, from a legal aspect, special cooporations of old market actors as well as innovative applications of old knowledge. Thus beside the general manufacturing questions the legal institutions seem to be tested too.

If a driverless car is to make an on-the-spot, or even a predetermined but externally generated, decision, for example, it needs to rely on special networks of databases, involving the questions of ownership rights, copyright and software issues, beside personal data protection and liability considerations. A driverless car, to be able to navigate on the public roads, needs data owned by a competitor, a driverless car's data one-two-three cars of it ahead, or needs to have access to others' special databases without the necessary legal relationship between the parties, resulting in, perhaps, the lack or in the end of the privity of a contract. Yet, vehicle to vehicle (V2V) and vehicle to infrastructure (V2I) communication may be rendered on a general duty of care in the traffic. But it triggers further concerns of protecting one's data, one's private data in a commission trip of the driverless car.

Obviously, the conception of property constantly changes. No one really thinks nowadays that without possession one could not have ownership, although possession used to be the bases of ownership: what I could possess, what I could grasp and protect should be regarded as mine. Hence come the tangible goods. The intangible things or assets, on the other hand, posit real headaches for lawyers even today. Intangible things, nonetheless, are vital to the business. Long before, came the copyholders of the land, then the shareholders in the company, which could be owned and thus became negotiable separately from others. Then even the "market position" as such was recognized as a unique subject matter of transactions thereby creating ownership and value. Afterwards the database was awarded legal protection, as a special asset, sui generis subject matter of the copyright and the civil law. And now the hottest debated issue is the ownership of the data in the clouds (Reed 2010).

These piecemeal changes in law basically follow the demands of the business and provide guarantees to assets there, where it is so desired by the market practices. Capitalism has always been built on information capital, thus on the efficient allocation of property of information, like business secrets, copyright, patent and know-hows (Cooter and Ulen 1989).

A self-driving car, however, generates further basic regulatory questions of robotics and law today. From a delicate legal point of view, there is an intriguing suggestion in the technology and law literature to consider (Calo 2015, Santosuosso – Bottalico 2016). Accordingly, depending on the nature of its purpose, task or function, an "intelligent" machine may be regarded either as a robot-object or a robot-subject. In a somewhat rude interpretation and summary, a robot-object, despite of its ability of information-transmission, qualifies as a thing in the eye of the law, if it is not autonomous. Autonomous in this respect would mean that the robot has independence, cognitive skills and special cognitive architecture too. Cognitive architecture would further include three special elements: teleonomy (special directed purpose), adaptiveness (capacity to adjust to the environment when challenged) and teleology (capacity to interpret the environment and adjust goals and means accordingly). Therefore, a targeting system, the argument goes, is still a robot-object, because of lack of independence: the ultimate decision is made externally, an operator pushes the "fire" button. Also, a landmine may well be independent, but lacks cognitive skills, since it explodes automatically when so programmed. A self-driving car, on the other hand, may rather be regarded as a robot-subject: (i) it is independent, it requires no external influence, (ii) makes independent decisions (iii) it has directed purpose, it understands its purpose and it is capable to adapt its actions to the environment, necessary for its goals to achieve. The final conclusion of this narrative is that the robot-subjects would be recognized differently in the legal context. Instead of calling it a thing, it would be a "non-human" agent, acting on behalf of the principal, let it be the owner or not. And in this latter case, the relevant applicable laws are different. In lieu of property and intellectual property or employment rights, products liability issues or consumer and data protection, the applicable laws or legal institutions here would rather be the agency problems, legal capacity issues, criminal law, torts, the non-contractual liability, e-personhood, intent, etc.

Consequently, driverless cars may be called also as tele-operated autonomous vehicles with cognitive skills. These cognitive skills, with special respect to the latest results in deep learning, allow better adaptivity and decision-making of own-account. Deep learning however, provokes further questions for lawyers: how to know whose software was bugged or whether it was the driverless car itself who generated the bug itself. So are these autonomous vehicles equipped also with cognitive architect, as the theory requires it from a robot-subject?

Definitely not, yet. Asserting that a robot can speak or answer the questions – even all questions – does not mean that the robot understands what it says. There are plenty of examples to that: Bina48 in the 1990s, Watson Jr. from IBM in the turn of the century/2000, or Sophia in 2018.

Driverless cars become robot-subjects, again, no matter what the rule is, when risk allocation rules for innovation so desire. The robot-objects are not at all in the visier of the law because they first need to qualify as a thing. A thing is defined by the legal literature. A general definition is that it has to be something that a man can keep under his control or power; even the wind, or the sun. As soon as the robot-object becomes more evolved, one could argue, and bursts out of this control, it becomes a robot-subject any way, even if the rules do not recognize it. Liability issues however are not at all the subject matter of pure moral and legal concerns, there can be plenty of examples to that, like the legal entity and liability or even culpability of a company.

The recent findings of neuroscience is that the free will, or the operation of a human brain maybe more pre-determined than it is generally accepted by the tort law or criminal law since at least the enlightenment (Scwaab 2014). So legal punishment might lose its ground and so it would put delicate questions to the law and robotics (Eszteri 2015).

Truly, these problems are not only legal questions but deeply rooted moral issues. The answers, therefore, more often than not, reflect one's own world view and one's tacit attitude towards legal norms as such, from a strictly legal point of view. If one accepts the view that the law is separate from any ethical concerns, than the law should be the matter of rational choice and economic interest beside the political deliberations. On the other hand, if it is not acceptable and one could not imagine a world without the moral foundations of the legal norms, then the answers to these challenges may lead to a very different path.

This chapter here, focuses on only a few of the problems, namely the privacy issues, the software issues and the strict liability issues.

3. The applicatory challenges by analogies

3.1. The applicatory challenge by analogies – Privacy analogies

The construction of privacy changes. Robotics in the driverless cars are desperately data thirsty. They need various enormous databases to be able to operate.

Thus driverless cars running on the streets often induce legal problems such as invasion of privacy, illegal data collection, illicit categorization and usage of them, to name but a few. Some of these include personal data, some infringe competition rules, copyrights or property rights of database-owners.

So what data and how should be protected?

The EU is highly sensitive to the personal data protection which is conspicuously demonstrated in the new General Data Protection Regulation (GDPR 2016/679). The idea of privacy by design (PbD) advocated in this piece of legal act is not at all brand new, it has been developed by the European Commission for some time, from the Privacy Establishing Technology project. However, the regulation itself was basically, though not entirely, triggered by the, allegedly, reckless use of the European citizens' personal data in the USA or US companies (e.g. Schrems v. Data Protection Commissioner C-362/14). The regulation has effect also outside of the EU in the sense that any company wishing to make any business in the EU but settled in a non-EET country should also comply (USA, China).

No doubt that both the European Union and the United States recognize privacy as a fundamental notion. The U.S. Constitution enshrines protection against state intrusions and the Charter of Fundamental Rights of the European Union (the Charter, art. 6-8) as well as the European Convention for the Protection of Human Rights and Fundamental Freedoms (the ECHR, art. 8) each mandate that law and public authorities are not to interfere with private life. Notwithstanding, lately, the state/police surveillance demands ever more invasion of these rights and a want for more data, due the recent indispensably data-addictivity of the new technologies and their reliance on mass businesses, and so allegedly mass security.

As one of the most influential judge, Richard Posner, in the USA puts it, "privacy is mainly about trying to improve your social and business opportunities by concealing the sorts of bad activities that would cause other people not to want to deal with you" (Posner 2014).

And this is perfectly demonstrated by the ECJ decision in the case of Gomez v. Google (C-131/12). The decision is wrong for its being as overbroad and over-inclusive as it is. Vesting a right in Mr. Gomez to claim a deletion of his data from Google generates serious problems with free speech and rule of law. In this case Google Spain had digitized a local newspaper in which, from that time on, if someone looked for an attorney in the region on-line in an advertisement, could bump into Advocate Gomez's house being at auction for overdue tax-depths. Upon Mr. Gomez claims the ECJ finally read the EU Treaty in a way, that Mr. Gomez was awarded the right to claim from Google to delete its link to his personal data. Hence there is a living right be forgotten in the EU.

Nonetheless, the right to be let alone advocated by Brandeis and Warren in 1890 was a conceptually diverging idea from the European right to be forgotten

(Brandeis – Warren 1890). The right to be let alone meant something else, though the leading case back then might resemble to the problem of Mr. Gomez. In this legal suit Ms. Roberson, an attractive girl had had a picture made of her at a professional photo shop and in a short while she realized that her so taken picture covered the paper package of the flour in the relevant grocery shops all over New York (Roberson v. Rochester Folding-Box Co., 71 N.Y.S. 876, 876 (N.Y. App. Div. 1901). Although the majority was in favour of the photographer, there was a powerful dissent in the decision of the New York Supreme Court, even citing the famous Brandeis-Warren article on privacy. Yet, this case emerged with the rising new technology of the smaller, portable photo camera allowing photographers to take pictures from anyone anytime anywhere, looking at the techniques of that time with a hindsight, and watching the then still man-size photo-cameras, this fear of invisible invasion of privacy by photographers must have only been a threat. However, the impression of the invasive being of photographers must have been felt real, because the new ever smaller and better versions of cameras came into the market so rapidly, that the threat must have felt very imminent even then.

Notwithstanding the internet, the crucial similarities in these two cases, more than a 100 years in between them, are that the actor who publishes or who decides to publish certain personal data is not the "owner" of the personal data. And this actor, thanks to the technical facilities, may act independently. It should be noted though, that in the early case of Ms. Roberson there were no copyright issues in the USA, whereas nowadays this aspect is not negligible at all. Ownership rights in Cyberspace, or the ownership in information is quite an important topic, since several of the basic elements of the term ownership are missing, namely the classical "thingness" of the object of the ownership and the exclusivity, or the exclusive use, of the owned "thing" (Reed 2010). On the other hand these cases show the huge difference in scale, in huge public access, which may matter the most.

Truly, the term privacy has problems and there is a discrepancy between the EU and the USA (Reidenberg 2014). Europe supports privacy even at the expense of free speech, and commercial speech too, which is the language of the business communication, the freedom of advertising and marketing. The USA does just the opposite. And indeed, legal privacy has many ramifications (Gormley 1992) and the construction of those may not always match between the American and the European one. Firstly, there should be the right to have secrets from the State even (laws against unwarranted searches), secondly, the right to have own opinion and to let it be public (free speech), thirdly, the right to be let alone (tort laws, damages by delicts), and fourthly, the right to have fundamental decisions (rule of law principles, fair hearing, fair trial). In addition, the new kind of business-models enabled by the new technologies provide further privacy issues, like the cross-border jurisdictional legitimacy problems. Whereas Brandeis and Warren dealt with basically the right to be let alone, the legal problems generated by the new technologies nowadays embrace all privacy elements.

Now, when a driverless car wishes to travel through several cities or countries in Europe, it needs to have access to a lot of databases. It uses for example, official public databases when gathers information about the street facilities. Then it uses private databases for meteorological data or pictures of the artificial world in the human environment, or outside. It may have access to personal data too when reaches out to the clouds and collects information about the exact location of a person, depending on the driverless car's mission. And again, it uses information which is owned by someone else(s). In these instances the smart things full of personal data being used and stored in one's home might become a useful, but illicit?, resource to the driverless cars.

The prescribed 'privacy by design' in the GDPR may not necessarily be safe unless privacy is legally clarified, precisely described and expressed to the designers and the design is specified in due course and in due terms. First of all however, the GDPR is a general regulation and even if it is directly applicable, certain technicalities require further elaborations. Besides, these specificities needs to be provided by the relevant authorities of the relevant Member States according to the applicable EU directives, such as the e-Privacy directive. Encoding privacy requirements into software is obviously, not at all self-evident in the EU.

Koorps and Leenes criticize therefore that the entering into force of the GDPR and thereby the privacy by design, would not solve even the problems of the personal data owners (Koorps-Leenes 2014). According to their opinion this new regulation would not change the existing mode of operation and would not stop the pattern in which the industry tries "to achieve rule compliance by techno-regulation". The claim is, that what may be intelligible for a human, may not be as such for the machine, the driverless car.

The Turing test fails here. Even if this test can help to decide whether the other speaking party is a computer or a human, it cannot have any prediction whether this other party thinks or understands his doing as well. Searle has his relevant, even rethought, criticism with the Chinese room, in which a sole non-Chinese speaking human could answer Chinese questions with a dictionary and a grammar book without understanding the questions let alone the answers (Searle 1980). Should that now mean that the autonomous vehicle cannot be liable, and that the data collected by the driverless car on the street can be freely downloadable because it has no rights either?

A question, what data could be collected and under what purposes on the public roads, could therefore be very important. It could include to decide whether special human mental diseases may contribute to traffic accidents in the streets. Is it allowed that manufacturers collect data therefore on sensitive health issues for safety reasons or health preservation on the public roads? What is more, the transfer of such data may further create sensitive personal data infringement. In order to facilitate the designer to "translate" these kind of purposes and requirements into codes there are other possibilities. Instead of regulation by design Koorps and Leenes offer the regulation through communication (Koorps-Leenes 2014 9). IoTs and autonomous vehicles should use data for profiling as well, since they in fact support one's routine activities, which, again, on the other hand, is a sensitive issue in the GDPR. This to be done needs prior and clear understanding and consent and in case of circumstantial changing, the approval needs a renewal too. To translate these changes in time more thorough interpretation and understanding is suggested.

This structure of data protection does not sort out the question, though, citing Posner above, whether it would be such a problem, if certain personal data were less protected and more public, as it used to be prior to the capitalism.

Despite of its newer regulatory model of the GDPR, the very existence of the GDPR is an evidence of how the top bottom law making works in law and robotics. Advocates of the GDPR claim that this regulation is needed, because the bad practices should no longer be tolerated and thus the social conventions must be changed by the law, ultimately by legal sanctions. However, the GDPR could well create a rather administrative, check-the-box answers with a send-the-declarations or disclaimers- always-everywhere attitude.

On the other hand, designers come to the market with products, with carefully prepared regulatory design, fit in the legal framework of the laboratory times. With the shift in time, however and when they really hit the market, the law changes and so should the regulation by design again, which again, is not so trivial. Koorps and Leenes demonstrate it by referring to the simple and surely predictable problem of aging: a minor needs the approval of the parents in order to have consent to data collection, but how to monitor its changes?

Surely, laws on robotics require from lawyers the understanding of technological details. And this is the challenge the law faces and which may be described by the stealthy technologies which again would trigger a necessary interdisciplinary pragmatism (Calo 2015, Urquhart – Rodden 2017, Somkutas – Kőhidi 2017).).

3.2. The applicatory challenge by analogies - legal entity

Although it is a (statistical) fact that autonomous vehicles create safer public roads, still no one needs an extraordinarily vivid imagination to fancy how much damages an autonomous vehicle may cause, if something goes wrong, without any human interference. Certainly, as long as the machine follows the rule, the encrypted orders, it may not be held legally liable. But let's suppose that there is a fleet of driverless cars operated by a network of these cars. Is that sort of business enough for holding this network of autonomous vehicle responsible, even liable? If this business makes money, should the driverless cars also be able to make money?

Common sense, that to qualify as a legal subject, one does not need to be a natural person or a human being. And this is true the other way round, not all human beings are/were legal subjects. Good examples for the first are companies with or without legal personality, the state or its agency, like the authorities, ministries. And examples for the latter are slaves. Currently, "everyone has the right to recognition everywhere as a person before the law" (according to the UN Charter, Art. 6). Also as ius cogens, it is found in the Hungarian Civil Code as well (HuCC Articles 2:1, 2:4 on the legal capacity of a human person and Art 3:1 on the legal capacity, and the scope, of a legal person). Though "everyone" needs not necessarily be a human being, the preamble of the charter might be construed that way. A thing may be owned, a person acts and has self-consciousness about his doing it, about his doing it rightly or wrongly. Nonetheless not only (human) persons can cause changes to the environment, or damages for that matter. Frequent examples are animals, but plants or volcanos too, in fact.

It is a commonplace too that law is a social construction and as such, granting non-humans legal personhood (legal personality or legal entity) may be a matter of rational choice, depending upon the world view of the regulators though. For a historical analogy, companies acquired the title of legal entity geographically sporadically but almost always driven by necessity motivated by business considerations (Hansman – Kraakman 2000). Without a reliable, transparent registry, the creditors were finally awarded with the separation of the assets. In order to create a trustworthy business environment the assets needed to be separated, so that to enable the creditors to have access to the company assets without competing with other private creditors of the company owners. So the legal entity of a company was a good move, even so because soon the limited liability of the company indeed insulated the assets of the company not only from other creditors too but also from the owners and the private creditors of the owners. Credit became cheaper.

Legal personality therefore is not necessarily a moral issue. Legal personality or legal entity allows one then to be recognized by the law, so that any act of this entity be legally challengeable, have legal consequences. On the other hand this legal entity may have also access to the courts in case of its grievances. Under classical European continental law legal capacity to have rights and duties is to be distinguished from the legal capacity to act which may be denied from non-human legal entities constructed merely by the law (Smith 1928).

And so it is in the case of the companies. So is the legal capacity of a company limited, it cannot act on its own behalf. Needs an agent. Notwithstanding the limited liability of certain companies, the liability of the companies are recently extended to certain criminal activities. It means that the acts of certain employees, usually that of the management, can be attributed to the corporate entity, if this activity benefitted the company and the employee committed it as the manager of the company.

In any event this sort of development in legal thinking has ever been based on the economic interest, on property allocations. And so, even if it seems now to be a shift in the legal thinking, it is not. Such application of a fiction is not at all new and conceptually the ultimate sanction is an analogy. The termination of the existence of the legal entity may be parallel to the execution of the human person. The reason of attributing this (criminal) deed to the company is therefore a moral and a business concern rather than a legal one. Why should the company be able to get away with a tax fraud, for example, when the company had the benefit of the crime and also the collateral, perhaps, for the remedies.

The idea is that the borderlines in the fields of liability have become blurred, and there are no longer clear distinctions among the territories of the criminal and the civil law or the administrative law liability. But this is not that big a change under common law, even if it creates debates under the German civil law tradition (Bérces, 2015, Ligeti, 2002, Eszteri 2015).

The objective liability, the liability without negligence or intent is not at all a new legal institute. The idea, that it is not only the human that can cause harm is again not a new notion. These legal tools of interpretation, however, were designed to be applicable in environmental protection cases or anti-corruption cases and not for machines having impacts on humans' life.

And in this sense, there is a distinction. In the case of the AI, IoT or autonomous vehicle it is ultimately not the human whose action is being under scrutiny and then judged. Therefore, none of these cases raised as seriously the question of legal personhood as it is being discussed in relation with the IoTs nowadays.

The technological phases of the artificial intelligence (AI) obscure the borderlines of the development and so the level of capacity too. The legal capacity of these machines may be hard to fix. According to a widespread notion of conditions an AI needs to be conscious about itself in order to gain legal personhood. No doubt, it all leads us to the interpretation of the other minds problem and the predictions of others acting and doing. But neuroscience does use predictions very often even at courts, at criminal trials. And so does the judge at the court, the prosecutor and the police too (Garland ed 2004 116). Clearly, the widespread use of such technique may not qualify the method as good but certainly as something practical which cannot be replaced with something better, so far.

The breaking point in questioning of the legal capacity of an AI was provided by Lawrence Solum's highly intriguing and illuminating article in 1992 (Solum 1992). He wrote that, with due regard to the complexity of the issue, the answer needs to be a pragmatic one. So he put the question, whether an AI may be a trustee. Solum distinguished three different levels of an AI. Firstly, the AI absolutely routinely follows the rules/orders and serves basically as a huge library for the owner who actually makes the transaction with the AI's assistance. Secondly, the AI practically sorts out the business on its own and enters the contracts but needs the signature of the owner. And thirdly, the AI does everything alone. Solum's conclusion was that although the time was not ripe, there might come a turning point where the AI will claim for own perhaps constitutional rights: what would stop an AI to open up a Law Directory on line and commission a lawyer to represent him at the court. Nick Bostrom would certainly object, alleging that it is due to the construction, the architect of the machine, which disables a machine to "think" as a human (Bostrom 2003). Solum further argues that multiculturalism prevents us from denying this possibilities for non-humans and he predicts the necessary change in legal concept of the legal personhood.

Twenty years later, Koops, Hildebrandt and Jaquet-Chiffelle relying heavily on this article and on its findings concluded still that at the time being, a proper construction of the existing laws would suffice (Koops – Hildebrandt – Jaquet-Chiffelle 2010). After having screened and summarized the relevant new European (legal) literature, they argue that the laws are flexible enough and allows the interpretation of the laws on agency – however divergently in the USA and in the EU – to be applicable to the machines being built. On the other hand, they emphasize, that sooner or later, all of the researchers suggest modifications to the law and perhaps to the legal concept as well (e.g. Matthias 2008).

According to their model, which recommends also a three-step approach, in the short-term, at the starting point, the interpretation and extension of the existing law suffices (Koops – Hildebrandt – Jaquet-Chiffelle 2010 554.). At this level, in case of a legal transaction, the acts of the computer may be attributed to the owner/user as his general intent. In case of invalidity problems, if the computer buys more shares than should have the court would have no difficulty to decide on the intent of the owner as the intent of the human and not that of the "electronic agent", since agency rules may not yet be applicable. As a middle term, they argue for a limited personhood with strict liability. At this level agency rules could already apply, so the agents need to be registered as such in a public registry which could allow the contracting parties to find the identity of the agent's principal (555). Besides, they recommend the cautious introduction of a limited type of personhood for the e-Agent with a strict liability, so that the owner/user of the electronic agent may be found and be liable in its stead without questioning the intent. A further suggestion is that these electronic agents may receive a modest provision for their activities which may be a bases for an insurance fund in case damages occurred and they themselves may be found liable (in civil law only), mostly because the owner/user may not be located or they deny that they gave reason to the transaction be in their names. And finally or thirdly, when technology evolves further, the long term solution is a full personhood with "post-human" rights. Post-human rights would refer then also to that that this is not the "classical human rights" anymore. This should be the time though, when self-consciousness emerge. As a criticism to that smart future, it is argued too, that this sort of consciousness is rather facilitated by interconnectedness, thus not individual or "real". On the other hand, cognitive sciences pile up evidences to make us believe that "human identity itself emerges from distributed brain processes" (559.).

To translate it all to the autonomous vehicles, it is for sure, that so far we are at the threshold of level two and three. To attribute intent or mens rea to the driverless cars and let them prosecute or be prosecuted in criminal law, should have a long way to come so far. That would surely require a certain non-predictability or an intentional deviation from the rule, with purpose. That is not very likely yet. It is unlikely that a driverless car on mission to the airport to pick up a friend of the principal would go to the theatre instead to pick up the most celebrated actor in the region; and thereby causing a car crash in front of the entrance in the overcrowded street. However, strict liability in car accidents may be attributed to the driverless cars, since it does not demand the reasonable acting or the questioning of the reasonable care. Here there is no investigation into the proximate cause and thus the classical conditions like intent or fault, negligence or recklessness are not considered.

On the other hand due to the damages a driverless car may cause, the risk must be assessed and allocated efficiently in advance. The autonomous vehicles' liability therefore may be paralleled with the strict or objective liability of the companies (product liability) in private law and be based on a simple risk allocation mechanism and not on intent. It is not the punishment or the retribution which should count, but the desire for restitution, the restoration of the assets status quo. The restoration of the wealth distribution to the pre-accident status quo is a private law principle as opposed to the criminal law ones. So the question is to which model one reaches out. If this could cause a paradigm shift, then it seems, that the insurance lobby might object that, since with such a shift all could incalculably change.

3.3. The applicatory challenge by analogies – Software warrants and strict liability

In the case of an autonomous vehicle therefore liability issues may become somewhat complicated. Based on the three-step model of awarding legal entity to an AI an autonomous vehicle should linger somewhere between the second and the third phase, at best. That would mean that the driverless car could have a limited legal entity should be registered in a public registry and should be vested also with strict liability from the owner/user part. Driverless cars therefore should act as agents and their actions should create rights and obligations directly to the principal. Further capacities will definitely be awarded if liability on its own account will be more innovation-friendly.

In case of a car crash, the principal or the owner does not drive. This is not a big difference in most Member States in the EU, where strict liability laws apply in these cases, and, more often than not, the owner/operator of the car is liable, who might happen to be the driver but not necessarily. It can be so, since strict liability has no causal condition as in a negligent or intentional tort. Simply by operating a highly hazardous equipment triggers the stricter, non-subjective, liability. In other words in these accidents the driver/owner/operator/principal can hardly be exempted from liability if damage occurred.

On the other hand where negligent tort rules apply, like mostly in the common law, the driver himself is liable only if negligent and therefore the proximate cause of the accident has to be cleared and proven by the plaintiff in order to be able to collect. The defendant in these cases can be released if he shows that the car was defected. In the event however, that the car is autonomous, the driver is the car itself, so the manufacturer would be highly motivated to grant certain legal personhood to the driverless cars. Then the autonomous vehicle, as an electronic agent will be held liable. Should it be strict liability applied directly or should it remain a negligent tort?

In any event, the liability issues need to be determined on a case by case basis, regarding also the fact that with the driverless cars the software problems may override the hardware ones. And software failures are often harder to allocate but even harder to find the causal link with the necessary evidentiary standards. Like in the case of unintended acceleration software problems in certain Toyota types in the 2009, in which the victims of accidents managed to prove that the software of the breaking system had bugs. The case remained controversial until years later the management of the Toyota Company confessed lying. The criticism pointed out that the causal link between the admitted bugs in the software and the direct cause of the accident was not proven at the court and the jury was wrong. (Cummings 2017). "It is well known that nearly all non-trivial software has bugs. Furthermore, because there are virtually an infinite number of different ways of solving a non-trivial problem using software, one can often find many opportunities for criticizing software quality, sometimes using criteria that are highly subjective. As a result, the plaintiffs in a software trial can be expected to attack the defendant's software by looking for bugs and criticizing the software's quality. If they can find bugs, and show that more likely than not those bugs caused the accident, then they can establish causation. They can also use purported measures of software quality, which may be subjective, to argue that the defendant failed to fulfill their duty to provide software of sufficient quality" (Cummings 2017 1.).

Surely, the running of the driverless cars on the streets will trigger these sort of liabilities through the warranty problems of others' softwares, like the use of the free softwares and open source softwares. In these cases the risk and thus the liability questions need to be ascertained on a case by case basis and in case of doubts, the damages should be borne by those in whose interest the driverless cars were operated. The present rules on car crashes could well apply in the non-common-law countries, as said, where in such cases the strict liability is the rule.

Safety standards are a starting point in these cases, since consumer protection and product liability derives from the assumption that the product needs to be safe. But how safe? Obviously a driverless car is regarded as to be safer than a car without or nearly autonomous driving. So under common law jurisdiction the question is, if notwithstanding, there is an accident, then the manufacturer is liable if the driver is not at fault. Product liability consists of three elements: defect in the product, defect in the design and lack of warning or lack of instructions. To translate these into the software case, bugs should certainly qualify as defects in the software. In those autonomous vehicles though, in which the deep learning is a standard, a bug may not necessarily be programmed from the start but might have been learnt by the machine. In all these cases the state of the art defence may help out the manufacturer from liability. Since most of the car companies rely on many suppliers, the driverless cars contain various softwares from different manufacturers, embedded even. This makes even harder the proving of contributory negligence or the percentage of interaction in the operation of the hazardous equipment, the car, in the accident.

Additionally, the autonomous cars need data. These data, for cybersecurity reasons, are provided via separate, very quick Wi-Fi like facilities, like the DSRC (Dedicated Short Range Communication) in the USA, and, probably, 5G in Europe, especially in Germany. The data flow needs to be free from misunderstanding, misinformation and hacking. In case of misunderstanding the question is whether there is an interoperability problem, or the rival systems fail. In any event, the node needs to be found and decided where the faulty data came from. In-built cautious messages, designs, such as use 'break, if...', could release liability. There probably is a duty of care on the public roads among the actors, therefore, if there is a misinformation, then the sender of the information may be liable for negligence or fraudulent misrepresentation if he knew or should have known that the information was false. Besides, the receiver of the information needs to show reasonable care to rely on the information received and does not react if other information contradict, like an obvious change in the traffic order. Cybersecurity protocols require special verifications of messages and other protection but hacking remains an evergreen issue, the softwares have to be able to manage it. In the end special investigation is needed to find the very legal entity, the manufacturer, supplier, seller, repairer, owner or operator to be liable. Bugs existence needs to be accepted and the software so designed so that to react reasonably cautiously.

Despite of the Toyota case, software liabilities are generally privileged in the legal systems. In case of contractual breach, the damages are limited even above the standard of the foreseeability doctrine and in torts cases the rule of economic loss applies. These all serve the same purpose that purely economic damages cannot be recovered and that the costs of innovation be widespread. Softwares in Cyberspace are extremely intertwined and since robotics are often facilitated by/on the internet, the security of the softwares is a crucial point in driverless cars. It is because robotics, and especially the driverless cars, unlike the softwares on the internet, are designed to be active in the real space, thereby much easier and more possibly causing more physical harms.

The application of strict liability of either the driver, which can certainly be the driverless car itself according to the level two-three above, or the producer or the owner, is justified first of all because of the acceptance that there is no bug-free software and because the very existence of the bug in the software may be discovered only by use. Thus the real question boils down to the procedure or to the protocol to be followed by design in situations of emergency. It is important since strict liability might provide for exemption in cases where the accident is due to an unavoidable interference of an action from the outside of the scope of the operation of the hazardous equipment, the car.

4. Conclusions - The smart future

"Well, Senator, my position is not that there should be no regulation" said Mark Zuckerberg, the CEO of Facebook at the Senate hearing, in a dialogue with Senator Lindsey Graham (R-South Carolina) (CNET Joint Commerce and Judiciary Committee SH-216, April 2018).

Entering a search request into the search engine of the Google Scholar, one receives more than 2.660.000 findings for the technical term 'legal paradigm', even if there are only about 1% out of these, which really match the request. And this is so despite the fact, that the notion of paradigm, is not at all evidentially applicable in the social sciences or humanities, thus in the legal context. Thomas Kuhn used the expression of paradigm, without the adjective, primarily to describe and to understand the truthfulness of the various and sometimes contradictory scientific assessments of natural sciences. His point of view was definitely historical and argued that certain statements may well qualify as scientific in one paradigm and not at all as such in another paradigm. Paradigm, summarized rudimentarily, would mean a complex world in which scientific development is achieved with putting the tiny little verified puzzles of the whole picture together. A paradigm shift would be brought about, put it again very unsophisticatedly, when certain puzzles could not fit in and so they challenge the truthfulness of the entire picture.

But these sort of paradigms were meant to measure/commeasure sciences pure, which were computable or verifiable in its strict sense. Social sciences and humanities, on the other hand, are not based on calculations merely, even though economics, sociology, demography, statistics would so claim. In any event law, or legal studies, is evidence-based, uses interpretation, argumentation and reasoning, and it relies much much less on calculations.

But paradigm shifts, for their being a social construction too, sociologically may also be biased. Accordingly, the paradigm shift may be delayed or accelerated depending on the social embeddedness of the very advocates of the different puzzles fit or unfit into the relevant dogmatic picture of the existing paradigm.

Paradigm, nevertheless, may translate into a context: a context of rules and language, to simplify again. And if so, it may apply to the legal environment as well, since, in a way, law relies on reading and interpreting texts by using the rules of the language.

This chapter discussed the problem of paradigm shifts in legal thinking through the technique of analogies. It concluded that as long as the same interpreting tools, such as fictions, analogy, distinctions, etc., are applicable in the various incidents and the court cases, there is no paradigm shift in the normal science. The answer is upto the courts.

References

1. Aarnio A 1984 Paradigms in Legal Dogmatics *Theory of Legal Science* Springer Dordrecht Peczenik A, Lindahl L and Roermund B eds 176
2. Aarnio A 2011 *Essays on the Doctrinal Study of Law* Springer p 237
3. Bérces V 2010 A magyar büntetési rendszer reformjával kapcsolatos jogalkotási kérdések *IAS* pp 83-99
4. Bostrom N 2003 Are we living in a computer simulation? *The Philosophical Quarterly 53* 211 pp 243-255
5. Calo R 2015 Robotics and the Lessons of Cyberlaw *Cal. L. Rev* 103 p 513
6. Cooter R and Ulen T 1988 Law and Economics HarperCollins pp 645
7. Cox I and Wilfong G eds 1990 Autonomous Robot Vehicles Springer New York pp 477
8. Cummings D 2017 Was the Jury Wrong about Toyota's Software? How Questionable Testimony on Embedded Software Tipped the Scales IEEE Consumer Electronics Magazine pp 103-107 [DOI: 10.1109/MCE.2017.2684939]
9. Daithí M 2016 My Favourite Things: The Promise of Regulation by Design, JOTWELL
10. Deibert R et al 2010 Access Controlled – The Shaping of Power, Rights, and Rule in Cyberspace The MIT Press
11. de Vries U 2013 Kuhn and Legal Research. A Reflexive Paradigmatic View on Legal Research*: Recht en Methode in onderzoek en onderwijs 3 1 pp 7-25
12. Eszteri D 2015 A mesterséges intelligencia fejlesztésének és üzemeltetésének egyes felelősségi kérdései IJ pp 47-57
13. Fuglinszky Á 2015 Kártérítési jog HVG-Orac
14. Garland B 2004 ed Neuroscience and the Law. Brain, mind, and the scales of justice. Dana Press New York | Washington, DC
15. Gelén K ed 2017 Jog, innováció, versenyképesség. Wolters Kluwer Budapest p 172
16. Gillespie N 2014 Richard Posner: Privacy is "Mainly" About Concealing Guilty Behavior. Reason. Free Minds and Free Markets
17. Glancy D 1979 The Invention of the Right to Privacy Arizona Law Rev 21
18. Gookins E 2012 Achieving a Safe and Reliable Product. A Guide to Liability Prevention. ASQ Quality Press Milwaukee, Wisconsin p 145
19. Gormley K 1992 One Hundred Years of Privacy Wisconsin Law Review. WILR 1335
20. Graziano T 2016 Cross-border traffic accidents in the EU – the potential impact of driverless cars ipol studies
21. Hansmann H and Kraakman R 2000 The Essential Role of Organizational Law. Yale Law Journal 110 No 3 390-440
22. Hildebrandt M and Rouvroy A eds 2011 Law, human agency, and autonomic computing: the philosophy of law meets the philosophy of technology Routledge
23. Hildebrandt M 2015 Ambient Law, Smart Technologies and the Rule of Law 27 octobre 2015 Cycle de conférences octobre-décembre 2015 Le futur du droit : big data, algorithmes et robotisation

24. Homicskó Á ed 2018 Egyes modern technológiák etikai, jogi és szabályozási kihívásai. Acta Caroliensia Conventorum Scientiarum Iuridico-Politicarum XXII. Budapest p 223
25. Johnson D and Post D 1996 Law and Borders – The Rise of Law in Cyberspace. Stan LR 48 1367
26. Jürgen R 2013 Autonomous Vehicles for Safer Driving. SAE International p 142
27. Kiilunen V 2018 Autonomous Vehicles, Competence and Liability in the EU –Answering the Call of the European Parliament DOI: 10.13140/RG.2.2.10863.74403
28. Klein T ed 2018 Tanulmányok a technológia- és cyberjog néhány aktuális kérdéséről. Médiatudományi Könyvtár. 30. p 166
29. Koops B – Hildebrandt M and Jaquet-Chiffelle D 2010 Bridging the Accountability Gap: Rights for New Entities in the Information Society? Minn. J.L. Sci. & Tech 497
30. Koops B and Leenes R 2014 Privacy regulation cannot be hardcoded. A critical comment on the 'privacy by design' provision in data-protection law International Review of Law Computers & Technology 28 pp 159-171 preprint version
31. Leroux C and Labruto R 2012 Suggestion For A Green Paper On Legal Issues In Robotics – ELS issues in robotics. Researchgate
32. Lessig L 1999 Commentaries. The Law of the Horse: What Cyberlaw might Teach Us Harv Law Rev 113 pp 501-547
33. Ligeti K 2002 Az Európai Unió büntetőpolitikája ÁJT pp 73-97
34. Lunders C and Tarpley P 2017 Autonomous Vehicles, USA. in: Autonomous Vehicles, The Legal landscape of DSRC in the US, UK and Germany. NortonRoseFulbright p 7-11
35. Matthias A 2008 Automaten als Träger von Rechten. Plädoyer für eine Gesetzesänderung Logos Berlin Verlag
36. Murray A 2013 Looking back at the Law of the Horse: Why Cyberlaw and the Rule of Law are Important Journal of Law, Technology & Society Scripted 310
37. Murray A 2007 The Regulation of Cyberspace: Control in the Online Environment Routledge
38. Nagy Cs 2010 The Rome II Regulation and Traffic Accidents: Uniform Conflict Rules with Some Room for Forum Shopping – How So? Journal of Private International Law 6 1 pp 93-108
39. Parrish M 2016 The 2009 Toyota Accelerator Scandal That Wasn't What It Seemed
40. Patterson D and Moratti S eds 2016 Legal Insanity and the Brain Science, Law and European Courts Law and Neuroscience: revising the Legal Standard of Insanity Hart Publishing p 336
41. Pétervári K 2017 Autonóm járművek és jogi felelősség – a "Tesla" baleset; avagy ki vezet(het)i az autót Gazdaság és Jog 25. pp 31-34
42. Post R 1991 Rereading Warren and Brandeis: Privacy, Property and Appropriation. Faculty Scholarship Series.Paper 206
43. Reed C 2010 Information ,Ownership' in the Cloud Queen Mary School of Law Legal Studies Research Paper 45
44. Reidenberg J 2014 The Data Surveillance State in Europe and the United States, Wake Forest L. Rev. 49 583-608

45. Rudgard S 2011 Origins and Historical Context of Data Protection Law European Privacy IAPP publication
46. Russen Spears V 2008 The Case That Started It All: Roberson v. The Rochester Folding Box Company Privacy & Data Security Law Journal pp 1043-1050.
47. Sanitt A 2017 Autonomous Vehicles – The Legal Landscape of DSRC in the UK. in: Autonomous Vehicles, The Legal landscape of DSRC in the US, UK and Germany. NortonRoseFulbright p 35-40
48. Ṣantosuosso A, Goodenough O and Tomasi M eds 2015 The Challenge of Innovation in Law. The Impact of Technology and Science on Legal Studies and Practise Pavia University Press
49. Santosuosso A and Bottalico B 2016 Robotics and the Law: A European Perspective Autonomous Systems: Why Intelligence matters. Conference Lecture, München, Automatik Industrie 4.0
50. Sárközy T 2002 Büntetőjogi intézkedések a jogi személyekkel szemben? MJ pp 449-456
51. Searle J 1980 Minds, Brains and Programs. Behavioral and Brain Sciences, 3: 417–57
52. Smith B 1928 Legal Personality 37 Yale L.J. 3. pp 283-299
53. Solove D 2004 The Digital Pperson. Technology and Privacy in the Information Age NYU Press p 296
54. Solove D, Rotenberg M and Schwartz P ed 2006 Privacy, Information, and Technology, Aspen Publishers p 322
55. Solum L 1992 Legal Personhood for Artificial Intelligences, N.C. L. Rev. 70 pp 1231
56. Somkutas P and Kőhidi Á 2017 Az önvezető autó szoftvere magas szintű szellemi alkotás vagy kifinomult károkozó. In Medias Res 2 p 232–269
57. Stallman R 2002 Free Software, Free Society. Selected Essays, GNU Press. Free Software Foundation Boston, MA USA pp 230
58. Sundquist M 2012 Oonline Privacy Protection: Protecting Privacy, The Social Contract, and the Rule of Law in the Virtual World Regent Univ Law Rev 25 p 153-184
59. Swaab D 2014 We Are Our Brains. From the Womb to Alzheimer's. Penguin Books Ltd p 432
60. Tóth A ed 2016 Technológia jog – Új globális technológiák jogi kihívásai. Budapest p 294
61. Urquhart L and Rodden T 2017 Towards User Centric Regulation
62. Urquhart L and Rodden T 2016 Working Title: A Legal Turn in Human Computer Interaction? Towards 'Regulation by Design' for the Internet of Things Working_Paper_March
63. Van Egmond Van P, Nijkamp P and Vindigni G 2003 A comparative analysis of the performance of urban public transport systems in Europe. Int'l Social Science Journal 55 Issue 176, p 235-247
64. Wadhwa I and Salkever A 2017 The Driver in the Driverless Car How our Technology Choice will Create the Future Berrett-Koehler Publishers
65. Warren S and Brandeis L 1890 The Right to Privacy. Harvard Law Rev, 4, No. 5 pp 193-220
66. WIRED (2016/12).

67. Zittrain J 2006 The Generative Internet, Harv L Rev 119 p 1974
68. Ződi Zs 2017 Az információs társadalom legújabb kihívásai a jog számára – Horizontális platformok. Gazdaság és Jog 25. pp 27-30

Regulations

The USA

i. NHTSA: Policy (Guidance) of best practices for the safe design, development and testing of automated vehicles prior to commercial sale or operation on public roads, 2017.
ii. USA House Bill HR 3388 on "Safely Ensuring Lives Future Development and Research in Vehicle Evolution or SELF-DRIVE." 2017
iii. USA Senate Bill: S.1885 — 115th Congress (2017-2018) [Report No. 115–187]: "American Vision for Safer Transportation through Advancement of Revolutionary Technologies Act" AV START Act, 2017
iv. Autonomous Vehicles / Self-Driving Vehicles Enacted Legislation. (05.18.2018) NCSL, National Conference of State Legislatures, USA
v. California regulation 2014
vi. California regulation 2018
vii. US Department of Transportation: Fact Sheet: AV Policy Section I: Vehicle Performance Guidance for Automated Vehicles 2016 12687g2-091916-v1
viii. Federal Guidance on Autonomous Vehicles, Washington State, October 18, 2016

The EU - The European Parliament

ix. Motion for a European Parliament Resolution with recommendations to the Commission on Civil Law Rules on Robotics (2015/2103(INL))
x. Resolution of 1 June 2017 on digitalising European industry 2016/2271 (INI)
xi. Resolution of 18 May 2017 on road transport in the European Union; 2017/2545(RSP)
xii. Automated vehicles in the EU, EPRS briefing, January 2016
xiii. EU strategy on cooperative intelligent transport systems, EPRS briefing, September 2017
xiv. 5G network technology – Putting Europe at the leading edge, EPRS briefing, January 2016

The European Council

xv. Discussing the Commission Communication – Digitising European Industry Reaping the full benefits of a Digital Single Market COM(2016) 180 final, 20 April 2016, 8100/16

xvi. Valetta declaration by Ministers of Transport at the High-level Conference on Road Safety(Malta 28–29 March 2017) - Way forward /Valletta Declaration on Road Safety

The European Commission

xvii. Europe on the move: An agenda for a socially fair transition towards clean, competitive and connected mobility for all, COM(2017) 283 final, 31 May 2017

xviii. European Commission/European Urban Mobility: Policy Context. 2017

xix. Final Report Summary – ROBOLAW (Regulating Emerging Robotic Technologies in Europe: Robotics facing Law and Ethics), CORDIS, 2015

xx. Member States of the EU

xxi. Guidance, (UK) The key principles of vehicle cyber security for connected and automated vehicles. Published 6 August 2017

xxii. UK: Automated and Electric Vehicles Bill 2017-19, dealing notably with the issue of insurance for automated vehicles, House of Commons Library, 2017

xxiii. Directive on security of network and information systems 2016 –, https://assets.publishing.service.gov.uk/government/uploads/system/uploads/attachment_data/file/567242/national_cyber_security_strategy_2016.pdf UK version

xxiv. DE: Achtes Gesetz zur Anderung des Straßenverkehrsgesetzes vom 16. Juni 2017. Bundesgesetzblatt Jahrgang 2017 Teil I Nr. 38, ausgegaben zu Bonn am 20. Juni 2017

OECD - International Transport Forum

xxv. Automation of the Driving Task: Some possible consequences and governance challenges 20 July 2017

xxvi. Human Factors, User Requirements, and User Acceptance of Ride-Sharing in Automated Vehicles 20 July, 2017.

Chapter 2.

OBJECTIVE LIABILITY AND THE RISKS OF INTERNET[2]

The second chapter focuses on the internet. The internet connects two parallel but intertwined worlds: the on-line and the off-line. If softwares are defect on the internet, it has physical consequences in the real world. Due to its connecting nature, the internet inserts a third assisting party into all on-line transactions. The role of the traditional actors is blurred, and extra risks are to be dealt with. The question of competence and liability faces challenges. If one uses others' softwares or databases via the internet, it necessarily generates a global incompetence. What should one know about others' softwares, globally? The question is which software, under what legal regime could cause problems? The answer may not be simple for the operation of a robot, since plenty of different algorithms shared by various owners – but learning even by itself too, therefore capable of doing mistakes itself too – may twist the process of fact-finding. The chapter suggests that due to this trap of an endless process of tracing back to the origins of the problem may promote the idea of applying strict liability instead of fault-based liability.

1. Introduction

The Venezuelan Supreme Court operates via cloud computing from outside of the country and uses Skype from at least 4 different venues such as the USA, Panama, Colombia and Chile. "Since July 2017, the full tribunal in exile, as well as its executive committee, has been meeting in cyberspace" (Bloomberg Jan 2019). With the inclusion of the internet, what is new, is the speedy way of communications among the interested parties. The judges could follow the rules simultaneously, hold hearings, do research and publish their judgement instantaneously via the internet. But where do the information come from, most probably even sensitive data in these cases? How to reach the necessary databases from different countries? What if these data were in the clouds, meaning in a server somewhere not really transparent for the data owners or data holders? Under what jurisdiction are these data storable, locatable and accessible?

Is it so that the physical here and now, long ago the core elements of the legal thinking, are not going to be relevant anymore? And does this mean that the question of competence and the question of the governing law is going to face

[2] For an earlier version of this chapter see: Kárpáti, József ; Pázmándi, Kinga ; Pétervári, Kinga: Does internet trigger strict liability?: Stealthy technologies vs. stealthy regulations. In: Gál, Zoltán; Kovács, Sándor Zsolt; Páger, Balázs (eds.) Flows of Resources in the Regional Economy in the Age of Digitalisation : Proceedings of the 7th CERS Conference Pécs, Magyarország : Magyar Regionális Tudományi Társaság (2020) 671 p. pp. 542-556., 15 p.

challenges? Who and where, under what legal regime could act, commit a crime or become liable? Or, in this case, who and where could have authority to award a decision.

The answers may not be simple in many instances, for example, in case of the operation of driverless cars where there are plenty of different types of algorithms shared by various owners over the globe, stored and accessed in the cloud in different legal regimes. These data greedy technologies need the ever more popular cloud computing which guarantee safe use of statistically measurable data cost-effectively. But would the widespread cloud computing- caused borderlessness finally terminate territorialism, sovereignty even, or just the other way round, would it trigger stricter protectionism from the part of the nation states?

Clearly, it is tempting to make people believe that the new technologies bring about a paradigm shift in the legal thinking (Ződi 2018). However, there can be no direct answer to this question (Shapiro 1999). Undoubtedly, there are many changes in our contemporary, specific world which could generate the feeling of radical difference. But do they touch upon basic legal principles too? Or would profound changes or many profound changes cause paradigm shift?

Apparently, there are two camps discernible in this scholarly debate: a) the data exceptionalists and b) the advocates of business-as-usual (Schwartz 2018). The data exceptionalists perceive new technologies as disruptive to the longstanding notion of territorialism in law. Because one cannot even tell where the data are located or where one has access to them, they claim that the traditional connections have become blurred. On the contrary, the advocates of business-as-usual compare the cloud computing with cross border bank wiring or e-transactions and claim that the data in the cloud are nevertheless physical, somewhere locally accessible and even seizable.

No matter what the rule is, however, innovative robotic technologies are going to be overwhelmingly widespread. This is the meaning of the stealthy technology. Yet with the emergence of deep learning, the development of technology may become unleashed. Nonetheless, the regulations intertwined with robotics are again stealthy: most of the administrative procedures – or even petty court procedures – provide for self-executive law enforcement via on-line services, like the possible establishment of a company through the European e-justice portal in the EU. Still, the evolvement of the robotic technology may trigger unleashed regulations, like the over-broad data protection regulation in the EU (EU regulation 2016/679, GDPR).

The following chapter explores the origins of the legal tools applied or suggested to be applied to these special cases generated by the new disruptive technologies. As it's shown, all of the legal techniques used or suggested to be used were known in the course of the legal history, none of these are new, but perhaps their applicability of scale or their conceptualization is different. And though it seems that the internet has changed our concept of time and location as applied in law, this chapter hopes to prove that the real change occurs somewhere else.

The internet introduces an extra – virtual – actor in all activities carried out through the web. This insertion of extra, third or fourth actor prompts further twist in the liability chain in the use of the internet. This twist with the internet then makes the typical relations to result in a several party level-playing field. The software, the hardware and the human activity connect via the internet and it applies a further link in the liability chain also raising thereby new risks in the given legal relations. As more and more databases are going to be used because of the greed for data, for statistically definable data, the liability for others' softwares or the liabilities for the contents of the various databases become undistinguishable. Whom – or what? – to make accountable for example if a map register fails to be updated leading to car crashes? Should there be immunities available for those who employ reasonable care or should there be objective liability regardless of the fault of the parties? Should there be limitless damages or should the boundless amount of damages be limited?

2. Stealthy Technology and Stealthy Regulation

The stealthy technology may challenge all these aspects of the law. Internet may diminish the difference between centrum and periphery in the sense that all information is available everywhere, non-exclusionary, at once. People get access via the internet to the same information simultaneously and instantaneously – ideally, at least. Nevertheless, not even the challenges prove to be new ones. The challenges are in fact three-fold: i) the protection of data from illicit intrusion or from unauthorised changes and usage, ii) the safeguarding of those data to be stored undistortedly and correctly, free from misunderstanding, misinformation and hacking and finally iii) the guarantee of proper access to these data. And besides, above all, the exact logging of these activities.

Cloud computing enables service providers to shift data swiftly from one place to another if space or energy efficiency requires so. This includes cross-border transferring of databases, thus creating a possible conflict of laws in case of legal disputes.

Smart cars, not only driverless cars, running in the streets may induce this sort of legal problems very easily. Their greed for data may result in invasion of privacy, illegal data collection, illicit categorization and usage of them. Some of these include personal data, some infringe competition rules, copyrights or property rights of database-owners. And if these data are in the cloud, as it is going to be more and more the standard, then special patterns of access need to be designed (Bradshaw et al 2010). So, what data and how should be protected (Currie, Seddon 2014)?

Due to the stealthy technologies, there are two discernible paths for that at the moment, both of them use the good old tools of the legal thinking: the legal analogies or fiction. These are (i) the classic protection of things, even if they are distinguished between property rights or privacy rights to the information or (ii) the use of special cloud computing models developed fairly recently.

The justification for granting ownership rights in the data derives from the basic desire of all data-holders to have control and exclusive access to those data. Doubtless, there is no need to demonstrate the eagerness how one downloads everything one likes, let them be music, book, picture or whatever else. This propertisation of the data, however, is fairly contested in the academic debates. The gist of the critical argument is that if data were to be propertised then there should be a market for that. And if there is a market then even data would further the difference between the haves and the have-nots (Pollack 2019).

The efficiency of these technologies requires further facilities, like cloud computing (Robinson et al 2011). As the popularity of the cloud computing grows, so grows the number of its versions. Recently there are three basic models: a) the Data Shard, b) the Data Localization, and c) the Data Trust cloud computing model (Schwartz 2018).

The Data Shard model provides for a multinational location to the companies. In this case automatism is involved and even a single file can be so broken and stored that the pieces end up in various countries as deemed to be the most efficient. Theoretically this model is the archetype of the cloud computing, in which the cross-border localization of the pieces is not easily definable. This model gives the data exceptionalists the real headache. In contrast to the Data Shard model, however, the Data Localization model guarantees that the data are stored in one place, in an entirely localizable manner, under one jurisdiction. The information is stored in one single country or a region. For example, the regional cloud services offered in the EU by Amazon Web Services or by Microsoft are not accessible from the US. And finally, in the Data Trust model there are two separate entities: the Data Manager and the Data Trustee. This separation guarantees that the Data Manager can only oversee the network hardware and software whereas only the Data Trustee can access the data exclusively. This cloud version enables both extraterritorial location of information and an extraterritorial access to it. An example for this is the Microsoft Cloud Germany with T-Systems Germany (Schwartz 2018).

As is seen, there are already several, even technical solutions to the problem of legal territoriality. Beside these answers to the stealthy technologies, the regulatory answers to the unleashed technologies are rather the strict liability rules as to be shown here.

3. Internet as the Virtual Assisting Actor

The use of the internet may be a clear example for unleashed technology. Because beyond the only seemingly, paradigmatic changes brought about by the internet, the most radical ones lie somewhere else. For in all relations which are administered via the internet there is an extra actor, an assisting party, involved. Internet connects. One accesses the internet so that to use others' softwares or databases. But this connection inevitably results in the involvement of the internet as an extra actor. And it has three fundamental consequences: (i) the assurance of a global virtual standardization, (ii) the assurance of a global physical standardization and (iii) the problem of widespread incompetence.

3.1. The Assurance of a Global Virtual Standardization

Prior to the industrial revolution there was no general physical standardization at all. The post-industrial revolution times however witness a physical type of standardization. In fact, it is not total whatsoever, since this standardization has been achieved in the real world. That means that the productions exist in the physical world, therefore there are always here and now. Yet this fixation in time and space inevitably allows deviations from the standard according to the needs of the specific circumstances. This technologically, economically, legally and culturally predetermined environment naturally impedes standardization globally.

But now, the internet grants the possibility of a total, global standardization, at least theoretically. The difference between the center and the periphery ceases to exist, because ideally at least, anyone can have access to the data simultaneously and instantaneously. There are products or services available now on the planet which need not have specific traits to be usable in special circumstances. Word processing or excel spreadsheets do not require specificities. In the recent period of industry 4.0 the unique characteristics of the products or services are not necessary. The problem of complexity is now the compatibility.

This sort of standardization may undoubtedly sound naïve. And indeed, for the privatization (Jeet Singh 2010) of the internet in 1996 naturally led to the protection of the national security requirements all over the globe even if this only reason is not necessarily equally applicable to all countries (Lehr et al 2019). Thus, the stealthy, yet soft regulations end up in the unleashed, sometimes particular, regulations.

Notwithstanding these new born deliberate localizations again, the theoretically available global standardisation triggered by the ubiquitous internet, creates further distinctions. The software is connected to the internet and so accessed by the car. Internet connects in order to use others' softwares and databases. If something goes wrong, who is going to be responsible or liable then? And so, this insertion of an extra actor renders an extra layer to the liability chain. It is inevitable. Clearly, this model of relationships on the internet disrupts the concept of the privity of the contract, namely that a mutual agreement could have effect only on the parties to this agreement. Third parties may neither be beneficiary nor be held liable, unless expressly stipulated so, in the contract or by the governing law.

However, the internet provides for a level playing field for the hardware, the software and the human action. What is more, the human action is not even indispensable anymore: the broker algorithms, bank transactions or certain robots, semi-autonomous self-driving cars exclude the human interference whatsoever. The actors are not liable in its traditional sense, due to lack of intent, the mens rea. The liability pattern of this sort of relationship certainly requires new aspects of the use of others' softwares and databases.

And this might (should) have impact on the relevant regulations. On the one hand, these uses of others' softwares or databases need rules, be it contractual or regulative. And on the other hand, these softwares and databases need protection as well. Since the purposefully switchable use of the various databases may demand the re-definition of the ownership and the investment interests or the use of robot algorithms (Leistner 2018).

3.2. The Assurance of a Global Physical Standardization

The current problem with the internet, from this point of view, is that an off-line and an on-line world co-exists. But this is not merely a parallel existence but they intertwine. The deficiency of a software product is tangible, has consequences in the physical world. A software driven defect in the braking system of a car may jeopardize life and limb of many on the roads. In all these cases the responsibility may be fact dependent, of course, but legally may not. It is certainly governed by negligent torts based on fault-liability in the common law systems (USA, UK), but not so in the European continent, where strict or objective, non-fault liability prevails.

Under the continental European solution, the decision in this case would not change a lot, since normally it is not the driver who is liable, but the operator/owner of the car. So, no fault of the driver needs to be proven by the injured plaintiff. In order to be exempted from this liability the owner/operator of the car has to be extremely cautious to avoid the accident, for even the defects in the car would not excuse them. The layers in the liability chain would however grow, and so would the blind liability, if the car needs to be linked to the internet due to lack of necessary space for the data.

On the other hand, in the case of negligent tort in the USA one has to act reasonably, with due care, and if it is shown, one is released from liability. Thus, one cannot neglect any default if perceived. If not perceived, that would be unreasonable negligence and if the proximate cause is established, it would draw legal liability with itself. If the user of the product realizes that something goes wrong, has to react on that perception. It is a duty. The car needs to be slowed down or even stopped. Without making sure that the problem is eliminated, the problem needs to be tackled with. This is the law of negligence in torts, or non-contractual derelicts. If the driver was not negligent then the product liability of the car producer or the software producer needs to be proven.

Yet, if the internet is involved as a third assisting actor, one may not have perception at all. One has no idea whether there is something wrong going on or not. The software or the driving of a car via the cloud computing may not allow human interference, often for safety reasons. Also, for safety reasons, there are special distinct fit-for-purpose computers, also known as robots, or smart cars for example. Owe to the application of the software via the internet, the different question of liability occurs in driving a car. Who is responsible: the hardware, the software or the driver? Or, in legal terms, the product manufacturer, the software producer (SaaS in cloud computing) or the driver (owner or operator)?

3.3. The Problem of Widespread Incompetence

And, from a legal point of view, here comes the third, and perhaps the most important consequence of the internet as an extra assisting actor being involved in these relations: namely the problem of widespread incompetence.

An abrupt total automatic switch off of the electronic devices in the moving car driven by specific softwares may cause damages, harm or immediate death. As seen, this may come, in the near future, as a total surprise, without any human interference or knowledge. Where there is incompetence from the part of the user, the question is: in what way should he be liable, since there would be no way the driver/operator/owner could have had acted so that to avoid the accident. He could only show diligence and best effort by bringing the car to the service station regularly, for example.

On the other hand, if someone operates a product over which he has no full power, but has nevertheless the interest in doing so, should bear the risk of possible damages. Simply by operating a highly hazardous equipment triggers the stricter, non-subjective, liability. In other words, in these accidents for example, the driver/owner/operator can hardly be exempted from liability if damage occurred.

Interestingly enough, it was exactly the time of the industrial revolution, when the opposite of the objective liability, the subjective liability was introduced. As the children of the enlightenment and free will, the legislators gradually enacted the so-called subjective liability, meaning that the individual responsibility is grounded on the intents or the will and the deeds of the person. An individual is free and acts in accordance with his free will and intents, therefore any damage caused by him may be righteously borne by him too. Since this notion included total indemnification, this kind of liability proved to be an obstacle to the technical/technological development. The loss or the injury which could have been caused, for example, by the railway companies could well have exceeded the profits. The objective or strict liability however is a limited liability in the sense that it does not contain all damage, especially not the consequential damage, but in exchange for this easement, objective liability applies even if one is at no fault. This sort of legal institution is a mere risk allocation.

This involvement of the internet in these relationships render special emphasis on data safeness. Who should warrant that the data given in the used database are correct or undistortedly stored and applied? Who should account for a due logging so that the identity, the time and the place of any possible access or change to the given database be traceable later on (Djemame et al 2013). These questions to be answered demand further distinctions and an analysis of the deeds of the various actors involved: the data provider, the internet service provider, the data user and/or ultimately the customer who might not be the data user.

3.3.1. *Incompetence from the Part of the Data Provider of Others' Softwares or Databases*

The data provider or perhaps a database owner need not be an expert as the US case of the mushroom picking laymen shows (Revolidis, Dahi 2018). In this court case the plaintiffs wanted to pick and eat wild mushrooms so they had bought a mushroom encyclopedia. But after having the meal they got so sick that they needed a liver transplantation (Winter v. G.P. Putnam's Sons (1991). Defendants were the publishing company for publishing others book though. The liability question was twofold: the deficiency of the book itself and of the content therein. Since the book was other publishing company's book and it was not defect, the defendant was not liable for printing others' book. The reasoning included the problem of liability of publishing houses for reprinting others' books. The argument of the court may be rational and acceptable, even if it is hard to digest that an encyclopaedia need not be correct. But what sort of data become obsolete? And when? And finally, what is more important: to have more information or to have checked information? Checked by whom?

Yet, the emphasis here is on the data or information of others. Internet connects and so generates global incompetence. For how to trace back the bad signals, the misinformation or misunderstanding or even hacking, in the interconnections of the various databases and softwares used throughout the internet causing defect in the services. Certainly, these softwares and databases have in-build protecting protocols but so far we live with the recognition that there is no bug free software. Can disclaimer be applied in case a map becomes unduly un-updated or a traffic code sign becomes obsolete? And could this be the case in the internet and especially in the case of driverless cars, for example?

Surely, disclaimers may be applicable among the producers or the suppliers themselves but it would work doubtedly in the consumers protection world. Regulation is going to prevail in this latter case, at least in the European continental legal regime.

3.3.2. *Incompetence from the part of the Service Provider*

The service providers' liability has been a struggle ever since they exist. So far, a service provider is not liable for the illegal content uploaded by the users of the internet platforms or other devices. Because service providers do not owe strict liability, their liability is fault-based, and there can be no way, that all uploading be censored in advance. So they have to be told, and so they are responsible in a case by case basis. In case of justified warning the uploading has to be taken down. If they knew or should have known that the uploading was illegal, they are liable according to the so-called notice and take down standard. This policy is still in effect – see Youtube, Facebook, Google etc (Tan 2018), – since at the moment not even the latest EU copyright directive, EU Directive 2019/790, has changed – or rather could change – this approach (Lendvai 2019). Nonetheless it is not at all bad news, since one should not promote institutional (let it be governmental or private) censorship and especially not at the expense of freedom of expression or the right to be informed.

The right to be forgotten policy enforced in the EU by the, wrong, decision of the CJEU (C-131/12, González) provides for a good example of how burdening this content liability may be. Service providers are literally given the right to constrain free speech. Besides, since internet is ubiquitous, deleting information in a specific jurisdiction will not necessarily bring about the cancellation of those data completely globally from the internet, as the case of the fight between Google and France demonstrates (C-507/17 Google v. CNIL). Nonetheless, such localization of the internet, at least in the Euro-Atlantic world, should fail, according to the AG and other advocates and supporters of Google in this law suit.

3.3.3. *Incompetence from the part of the Data User Other than the Customer*

The problem of competence regarding the data users other than the consumers embrace the good old issues of suppliers' product liability. Products must be safe, producers as well as suppliers have strict liability in this matter.

By the assistance of the internet, however, suppliers are often software producers or database owners. The smart, semi-autonomous or driverless cars reach out for data from the various databases located and accessed probably in the clouds. Yet, in contrast to the protection of the databases from illegal intrusion, the running of the driverless cars on the streets will trigger the problem of liability issues through the warranty problems of others' softwares too. These may well stand for the use of the free softwares and open source softwares. But how to tell which data are bugged and who should be liable. With the problem of deep learning this conundrum is going to get ever trickier finally rendering the user incompetent.

In any event, software liabilities are privileged ones. The liability is strict, but there always is a cap on the amount of compensation.

3.3.4. *Incompetence from the part of the Data User, as ultimately the Customer*

Finally, the customers are, by definition, exempt from the need of being an expert. Notwithstanding because of the interconnection via the internet, internet adds another layer here too into the liability chain while blurring the traditional thresholds of human actions. As robots or algorithms take the place of the human steering, customers are no longer going to be the real actual drivers, not only because of the lack of understanding of the machine as has been the case for some time, but because of the actual exclusion of the human action by the robots.

Due to these concerns, it is intriguing to consider whether or not the application of strict liability is fairly justified. Clearly, in order to preserve the safety of the usable databases and the safety of others' softwares the actual legal solution is a sheer risk allocation rule.

Yet, if this is all only a risk allocation rule, then strict liability draws with itself the necessity of the insurance liability. These sort of insurance policies however do incorporate limited liability again. Theoretically software defects in the internet may by chance wipe out map information perhaps causing tremendous unthinkable damage. If there were no limit on these instances, there were no innovation in the first place. But weren't there really (Keren-Paz et al 2019)?

4. Strict Liability - or the Case of the Softwares in the Driverless Cars

Strict liability is thus a kind of objective liability. It is basically an application of a fiction. It allows us to use a narrative of a situation which we know is not true. In these cases one interprets the law upon the facts: "as if".

In case of a car crash, the operator or the owner does not drive. In most Member States in the EU, this is not a big difference, where strict liability laws apply already in these cases, and, more often than not, the owner/operator of the car is liable, who might not necessarily happen to be the driver. It can be so, since strict liability has no causal condition as in a negligent or intentional tort. Simply by operating a highly hazardous equipment one triggers the stricter, non-subjective, liability. In other words, in these accidents the driver/owner/operator can hardly be exempted from liability if damage occurred.

On the other hand, where negligent tort rules apply, like mostly in the common law, the driver himself is liable only if negligent and therefore the proximate cause of the accident has to be cleared and proven by the plaintiff in order to be able to collect. So the injured plaintiff needs to show that the driver was at fault. The defendant driver in these cases can be released if he proves that the car was defected. In the event however, that the car is autonomous, the driver is the car itself and so the manufacturer would be liable citing product liability. Product liability is also a kind of strict or objective liability. But should it be the strict liability of the producer of the software or hardware applied directly or should it remain a negligent tort for the driver, for the manufacturer?

In any event, liability issues need to be determined on case by case basis, regarding also the fact that with the driverless cars the software problems may override the hardware ones. But software failures are often harder to allocate and even harder to find the causal link with the necessary evidentiary standards. Yet it can happen. Like in the case of unintended acceleration software problems in certain Toyota types of 2009, in which the victims of those accidents managed to prove that the software of the braking system had had bugs. The case remained controversial though, until years later the management of the Toyota Company confessed lying. Notwithstanding, the criticism pointed out that the causal link between the admitted level of bugs in the software and the direct cause of the accident was not proven at the court and the jury was wrong (Cummings 2017). "It is well known that nearly all non-trivial software has bugs. Furthermore, because there are virtually an infinite number of different ways of solving a non-trivial problem using software, one can often find many opportunities for criticizing software quality, sometimes using criteria that are highly subjective. As a result, the plaintiffs in a software trial can be expected to attack the defendant's software by looking for bugs and criticizing the software's quality. If they can find bugs, and show that more likely than not those bugs caused the accident, then they can establish causation. They can also use purported measures of software quality, which may be subjective, to argue that the defendant failed to fulfill his duty to provide software of sufficient quality" (Cummings 2017 1).

5. Use of Internet and the Liability for Softwares in the Driverless Cars

As smart cars travel on the roads, or most importantly, in the cities, the risk and thus the liability questions need to be ascertained on a case by case basis and in case of doubts, the damages should be borne by those in whose interest these cars were operated. The present rules on car crashes could well apply in the non-common-law countries, as said, where in such cases the strict liability is the rule. Strict liability is therefore the fiction: it means that unless proven otherwise – in a very narrowly interpreted situation – the lack of proximate causation is not going to be an obstacle to find the producer or the database owner liable; as if...

Safety standards are a starting point in these cases, since consumer protection and product liability derive from the assumption that the product needs to be safe. But how safe? Obviously, a driverless car is regarded to be safer than a car without (or nearly) autonomous driving. So, under common law jurisdiction the question is, if notwithstanding, there is an accident, then the manufacturer is liable if the driver is not at fault.

Product liability consists of three elements: defect in the product, defect in the design and lack of warning or lack of instructions. To translate these into the software case, bugs should certainly qualify as defects in the software. In those autonomous vehicles though, in which the deep learning is a standard, a bug may not necessarily be programmed from the start but might have been learnt by the machine. In all these cases the state-of-the-art defense may help out the manufacturer from liability. Since most of the car companies rely on many suppliers, the driverless cars contain various softwares from different manufacturers, embedded even. This makes even harder the proving of contributory negligence or the percentage of interaction in the operation of the hazardous equipment, the car, in the accident.

Notwithstanding, if the rule of negligence applies and so reasonable care must be shown, just like among the software producers the internet again inserts an extra link of risk into the relations. The data flow needs to be found free from misunderstanding, misinformation and hacking. In case of misunderstanding the question is whether there is a compatibility problem, or the different systems fail. In any event, the link has to be located and decided where the faulty data came from. Special protecting protocols or designs, such as the use of 'stop, if...', could release liability. There is a duty of care among the actors, therefore, if there is a misinformation, then the sender of the information may be liable for negligence or fraudulent misrepresentation if he knew or should have known that the information was false. Besides, the receiver of the information needs to show reasonable care too to rely on the information received and does not react if other information contradicts, like an obvious change in the traffic order. Cybersecurity protocols require special verifications of messages and other protection but hacking remains an evergreen issue, the softwares have to be able to manage it. In the end special investigation is needed to find the very legal entity, the manufacturer, supplier, seller, repairer, owner or operator to be liable. Bugs' existence needs to be accepted and the software so designed so that to react reasonably cautiously.

Despite of the Toyota case, software liabilities are generally privileged in the legal systems. In case of contractual breach, the damages are limited even above the standard of the foreseeability doctrine and in torts cases the rule of economic loss applies. These all serve the same purpose that purely economic damages cannot be recovered and that the costs of innovation be widespread. Softwares in cyberspace are extremely intertwined and since robotics are often facilitated by/on the internet, the security of the softwares is a crucial point. It is because robotics, and especially the driverless cars, unlike the softwares on the internet, are designed to be active in the real space, thereby much easier and more possibly causing huge physical harms perhaps.

The application of strict liability of either the driver, which can certainly be the driverless car, in the near future, or the producer or the owner, is justified first of all because of the acceptance that there is no bug-free software and because the very existence of the bug in the software may be discovered only by use. Thus, the real question boils down to the procedure or to the protocol to be followed by the design in situations of emergency. It is important since strict liability might provide for exemption in cases where the accident is due to an unavoidable interference of an action from the outside of the scope of the operation of the hazardous equipment, the car.

6. Conclusion

Despite of the all-encompassing disruptive nature of the newest technologies, clearly, as is shown, there always is a pre-digital analogy for any rule, no matter whether they are stealthy or unleashed. Recent innovations include stealthy technologies as well as unleashed ones every now and then triggering stealthy and sometimes unleashed regulations. In fact, however this should not be wondered, since these technological changes would not be called innovation if the rules were not to be challenged. For what is the point in those innovations which could fit in a rule having been visioned for some times in the past as fit to the future of then (Mehra and Trimble 2014).

Internet however does have a special new feature. Internet connects. Internet creates two parallel but intertwined worlds: the on-line and the off-line world. And by enabling ones to connect and use others' databases and softwares, the internet generates global incompetence. If softwares are defect on the internet it has physical consequences in the real world. With its connecting nature, internet inserts a third assisting party into all on-line transactions. The role of the traditional actors is undistinguishable and extra risks triggered by the internet are to be dealt with. The question of competence and liability faces challenges. One uses others' softwares or databases via the internet.

This chapter hopes to have demonstrated that the notion of strict liability towards the consumers for the use of others' softwares or databases on the internet is a welcomed and efficient risk allocation rule. It is so, because otherwise one gets into a trap of never-ending tracing back to the origins of the problems in software bugs. Softwares in cyberspace are extremely intertwined and since robotics are often facilitated by/on the internet, the security of the softwares is a crucial point. The application of strict liability of either the driver, which can certainly be the driverless car, in the near future, or the producer or the owner, is justified first of all because of the acceptance that there is no bug-free software and because the very existence of the bug in the software may be discovered only by use. Owe to the problem of the extended incompetence prompted by the internet and shown above, the application of strict but limited liability for softwares may be a fair bargain.

References

1. Bradshaw, S., Millard C., Walden, I. 2010. Contracts for Clouds: Comparison and Analysis of the Terms and Conditions of Cloud Computing Services. CCLS Legal Aspects of Cloud Computing Research Project. Queen Mary University of London, School of Law. Legal Studies Research Paper No. 63/2010. Electronic copy available at: http://ssrn.com/abstract=1662374
2. Cummings, D. 2017. Was the Jury Wrong about Toyota's Software? How Questionable Testimony on Embedded Software Tipped the Scales IEEE Consumer Electronics Magazine pp 103-107 [DOI: 10.1109/MCE.2017.2684939]
3. Currie, W., Seddon, J. 2014. A Cross-Country Study of Cloud Computing / Policy and Regulation in Healthcare. Complete Research. Twenty Second European Conference on Information Systems, Tel Aviv
4. Djemame, K., Barnitzke, B., Corrales, M., Kiran, M., Jiang, M., Amstrong, D., Forgó, N., Nwankwo, I. 2013. Legal issues in clouds: towards a risk inventory. Philosophical Transactions: Mathematical, Physical and Engineering Sciences, Vol. 371, No. 1983, e-Science-towards the cloud: infrastructures, applications and research (28 January 2013), pp. 1-17 Published by: Royal Society Stable URL: https://www.jstor.org/stable/41739965
5. Jeet Singh, P. 2010. From a Public Internet to the Internet Mall. Economic and Political Weekly, Vol. 45, No. 42. 16-22 pp. URL: https://www.jstor.org/stable/20787466 Accessed: 03-07-2019 07:15 UTC
6. Keren-Paz, T., Cockburn, T., El Haj, A. 2019. Regulating innovative treatments: information, risk allocation and redress, Law, Innovation and Technology, 11:1, 1-16, DOI: 10.1080/17579961.2019.1572701
7. Lake, E. 2019. The Exiled Court Protecting Venezuelan Democracy. Judges meeting via teleconference bolster the constitution and the legitimacy of Juan Guaido. BLOOMBERG Politics & Policy. 2019. 01. 28
8. Leistner, M. 2018. Big Data and the EU Database Directive 96/9/EC: Current Law and Potential for Reform Available at SSRN: https://ssrn.com/abstract=3245937 or http://dx.doi.org/10.2139/ssrn.3245937
9. Lehr, W., Clark, D., Bauer, S., Berger, A., Richter, P. 2019. Whither the Public Internet? Journal of Information Policy, Vol. 9, pp. 1-42 URL: https://www.jstor.org/stable/10.5325/jinfopoli.9.2019.0001 Accessed: 03-07-2019 07:13 UTC
10. Lendvai, Z. 2019. Controversies Around the New Copyright Directive. Budapest Business Journal, 21 June. https://www.bakermckenzie.com//-/media/files/insight/publications/2019/06/controversies-around-the-new-copyright-directive.pdf
11. Mehra, S., Trimble, M. 2014. Secondary Liability, ISP Immunity, and Incumbent Entrenchment. The American Journal of Comparative Law, Vol. 62, supplement, pp. 685-705. Oxford University Press https://www.jstor.org/stable/10.2307/26425415
12. Pollack, M. 2019. Taking Data. The University of Chicago Law Review, Vol. 86, No. 1, pp.77- 142 URL: https://www.jstor.org/stable/10.2307/26554393
13. Reed, C. 2010. Information "Ownership" in the Cloud. CCLS Legal Aspects of Cloud Computing Research Project. Queen Mary University of London, School of Law.

Legal Studies Research Paper No. 45/2010. Electronic copy available at: http://ssrn.com/abstract=1562461

14. Robinson, N., Valeri, L., Cave, J., Starkey, T., Graux, H., Creese, S., Hopkins, P. 2011. The Cloud Understanding the Security, Privacy and Trust Challenges. The European Commission. Directorate General Information Society and Media Europe. Rand Corporation
15. Schwartz, P. 2018. Legal Access to the Global Cloud. Columbia Law Review, Vol. 118, No. pp. 1681-1762. Stable URL: https://www.jstor.org/stable/10.2307/26511248
16. Shapiro, A. 1999. The Internet. Foreign Policy, No. 115 (Summer, 1999), pp. 14-27, URL: https://www.jstor.org/stable/1149490 Accessed: 03-07-2019 07:16 UTC
17. Tan, C. 2018. Application of the terms of service in: Regulating Content on Social Media Book. Subtitle: Copyright, Terms of Service and Technological Features URL: https://www.jstor.org/stable/j.ctt2250v4k.8
18. Ződi, Z. 2018. Platformok, robotok és a jog. (Platforms, Robots and the Law). Gondolat. Budapest. p.264

PART 2.

SOCIAL RISKS AND COSTS OF REGULATIONS

Chapter 1.

RISKS OF SYSTEMATICALLY UNKEPT PROMISES[3]

The third chapter is a case study, providing a possible interpretation of the current Hungarian financial-legal culture. The underlying question is how to apply those terms and conditions in long-term loan agreements in financial crisis, which are favorable or seemingly irrelevant in good times but turn out to be disadvantageous, sometimes even disastrous in bad times. In other words, how to calculate and allocate risks, what is acceptable and what is foreseeable to laymen? The focus here is on the laymen attitudes towards long-term contractual obligations and performances in the global financial crisis. Further questions include whether debtors' contractual obligations must be fulfilled, what should be construed as an excuse for non-performance, whether there should be measures designed to protect the debtors more: if yes, at whose expense – the creditors (through preventive measures) or the taxpayers (through restitutive measures) –, if no, how to allocate ideally the risks and liabilities, is profit-making an evil per se, that needs to be managed?

1. Introduction

This chapter is about a possible interpretation of the current Hungarian financial-legal culture amongst the students, especially related to the private credits and private loan agreements. It has been almost a decade since the latest financial crisis grew global. And although this kind of crisis – however different it may have been – is an immanent characteristic of capitalism, there is still a great deal of doubts and uncertainty in the reactions of the (Hungarian) people. How to apply the rules and conditions in the agreements which were favorable or seemingly irrelevant in good times but turn out to be disadvantageous, sometimes even disastrous in bad times. Should they be foreseeable? Foreseeable to whom?

The question whether there is such a thing like ethical economy (Griffiths – Lucas, 1996), has perhaps never been discussed so intensively and challenged so globally (Picketty, 2013), as it is nowadays. The motivation such as "greed is good" has perhaps never been to be hidden behind such a dense drapery. Besides, however, the series of questions of accountability or responsibility (liability)

[3] Special thanks should be devoted to András Bleyer, Professor of Mathematics, who was so enthusiastic about making sense of the data gathered through the surveys, and without whose help these tables below would not be so legible. This goes without saying, of course, that all responsibility for the possible misunderstanding or misinterpretation of these data is entirely mine. For an earlier version of this chapter see: Pétervári, K. (2018) "How to Keep a Promise: Laymen Answers to the Financial Crisis", Periodica Polytechnica Social and Management Sciences, 26(1), pp. 49–66. https://doi.org/10.3311/PPso.10427

emerge ceaselessly together with analysis, should they be legal (Pázmándi, 2015), political, ethical or cultural (Fleck-Gajduschek, 2015).

There is, certainly, nothing new in the problem of keeping a promise in adverse (economic) conditions. Hungary has also survived many wars, inflations, revolutions and turmoils[4]. The idea of pacta sunt servanda has long been a legal rule of civil law in Hungary too. So it is accepted, that the parties must perform unless the newly emerged (excusable, unforeseeable?) circumstances make it impossible for a party to fulfill the earlier promise, *clausula rebus sic stantibus*.

Obviously, the existence of such rules, such legal rules, require developed ideas about how individual and/or social risks are to be calculated and allocated (Hatzis, 2015). And further the existence of such rules does not necessarily mean that they are efficiently enforced or applied. The more such rules are part of a legal culture, the clearer it can be the kinds of events which may be unforeseeable (therefore excusable), really unexpected, and which are not. Lately, the widespread use of long-term private credits (the consumer loans, or the consumer loan agreements) offer good chances to illustrate what people in Hungary think about long term obligations, responsibility, calculations, financial risks, liabilities, performances and excuses. The relevant question in law is, how likely and how foreseeable the various possible new scenarios (e.g. a global economic financial crisis) or the (non-) expected human reactions – both biologically (e.g. serious illness) and sociologically (e.g. a divorce, or unemployment among – lower – middle class people) – could be.

Some of these considerations are inevitable, for the parties entering into a contract, to calculate the risks (in both sides) and thereby allocating the liabilities properly, in other words, to use resources efficiently. If special unexpected changes in the performance or in the circumstances are not foreseeable or not arranged in the agreement properly, then instead of the prior risk minimization rules, the liability for damages must be applied so that to offer efficient remedies[5].

The following chapter enquires the laymen reactions upon the above-mentioned situations. It analyses the laymen attitudes of the long-term contractual obligations and performance in the global financial crisis: (i) whether the obligations of a loan agreement have to be fulfilled no matter what new circumstances may occur, (ii) whether the original objective of the debtor in a loan agreement

---

[4] See e.g. the Hungarian Legal Journal (*Jogtudományi Közlöny*) between 1921-1923 for illustrating the problems of performance of long-term contracts under and after WW I.

[5] It should be emphasized, that the word "responsibility" here is being used in a much more broader sense than it is suggested by András Földi (Földi, 2004) in his book, reviewing (also) the historical conception of responsibility; This, perhaps a little bit overbroad, understanding of responsibility is naturally due to the goal of the questionnaire which is to interrogate the laymen so the respondents are non-law students, therefore their interpretation of responsibility or liability or accountability may not be so distinctive. Also that is why my construction of responsibility here purports to include "cultural responsibility" such as solidarity as well and horribile dictu risk and responsibility might well be used interchangeably, since they are – in certain sense – just the other side of the same relations.

makes any difference in case of failure, (iii) what kind of events should be construed as an excuse for non-performance, (iv) whether there should be measures designed to protect the debtors more, (v) if yes, at whose expense – the creditors (rather preventive measures) or the taxpayers (rather restitutive measures), (v) if no, how to allocate ideally the risks and liabilities, and finally (v) whether profit-making is an evil *per se,* that needs to be managed.

2. The methodology

The survey was conducted through several years (between January 2013 and September 2016) among the same, from a statistical point of view, homogeneous groups. The questionnaires were to be answered in every semester by the students of the business law course at the very beginning, in the first class. The students are therefore generally among 20-24 years of age and have presumptively different sociological and geographical backgrounds, of course. What makes them comparable though, is their age, their lack of interest to be a lawyer, but their aim to be engineers or economists, their being at the threshold of their professional life and basically their common educational culture at school. This generation was born after the Transition[6].

Naturally, the questionnaires are anonymous and non-obligatory. The total number of answers so received is close to 400. The survey seeks to have answers on these students' attitudes towards private expectations, private debts, private bankruptcies, possible state duties and therefore implicitly, about contractual obligations, market failures and perhaps solidarity.

A caveat should be emphasized here, though. Undoubtedly, several hermeneutical doubts may occur, as in any questionnaire, by answering the questions in the different cases or legal situations. Since the aim is to find out the laymen's reactions to the financial crisis, the various terms are actually used in their everyday common understandings, provided that there are any. So here there should be more scenarios (Pázmándi, 2015) to clarify.

First, when using the various legal terminus technicus which have no 'exact' correspondent terminology in the every day life, a broader lay-conception of the terms are to be understood. Thus, for example, there are no distinctions amongst the different long-term loan agreements, whether these cover a consumer credit construction or a lease purchase contract or a sales and purchase agreement. These are to be understood as long term binding obligations.

Second, there are certain legal conceptions which do comply with an everyday meaning but not necessarily to that one what the term would be used for. Consider, for example, the institution of private/individual bankruptcy, which was

[6] "Transition" here is meant to describe the democratisation and marketisation process of the post-communist societies after the collapse of the Soviet regime in East-Central Europe in the 1990s.

not even in the public discourse at the beginning of the conducting the survey (see fn. 9 and 11. below). Bankruptcy, as such, is foggy and pejorative in traditional Hungarian common discourse. It might refer to an unworthy release from debt, but could mean a cunning release from it too. Owe exactly to the very nature of this survey, that the students filled in these questionnaires without having had the chance to distinguish among the various institutions in the questionnaire, this private bankruptcy institution might represent different conceptions or have dubious and vague objectives for the respondents. In any event, this term might not give enough insight into its real meaning in the survey.

Third, in some cases certain pre-conception is already presumed on the part of the respondents. So for example, taking private loan for purchasing further real estates as an investment might qualify as private speculations for some, whereas business investment for others. As a matter of fact who can tell?

What makes a business to be a business, from a non-legal point of view? Also, the use of other somewhat vague terms, adjectives, like "luxurious" expenses, however relative their meanings might be, lack the prior clarifications or distinctions too, so they are used as common sense, whatever that might well be (see fn. 7. below).

3. The basic scenarios

The whole questionnaire has basically three different groups of questions. The first group of questions is A) what would someone do in case a private debtor (a consumer) fails to perform in a long-term loan agreement concluded for further three very different purposes: i) the purchase of a flat, ii) the purchase of a luxurious sport car or a luxurious vacation, or finally iii) the purchase of real estates as an investment. The second – here not to be discussed – group of questions B) concerns answers, like what would someone say if damage were caused at the workplace and the claim should be against a company (employer) or against an employee. The third group of questions C) deals with the attitudes towards business or rather business failures, and enquires whether the small and medium enterprises (SMEs) should be supported by any regulations steered by the state and eventually what sort of deliberative decision-making would be satisfactory for any business calculation.

The analysis of these data, received from the responding students and processed in a freely accessible PSPP database, provides for the following results.

The basic scenarios of the private long-term loan agreement and the answers pertaining to them are the following (3.1., 3.2., 3.3.). The very first questions of the survey are whether one would help someone else who is in failure of performing a long-term loan agreement, depending on the objective of the spending and the circumstances causing the default.

3.1 Saving for what?

According to the first scenario, in which a flat was purchased, the indebted person failed, despite of his precautious acting by having calculated possible risks and costs well before the decision. He has failed due to the global economic and financial crisis and because his employer was wound up so he also looses his good job. The majority of the answers voted for help. (yes: 63.13 % – no: 32.96 %[7]).

When the same question concerned a slightly different situation, namely, that the failure to perform was due to the fact that the debtor's wife got ill, and so needed more care that cost a lots of money and time, so he loses his job, the willingness of help even raise higher. (yes: 84.64 % – no: 11.73 %).

On the other hand, when the pay back of the loan is stopped because the couple decides to divorce and that proves to be too expensive, the helping intentions decrease dramatically. (yes: 20.95 % – no: 74.58 %).

So far it may be said that the respondents are quite sympathetic to the debtors. It is well accepted to use credit for buying a place to live in even if one is without the means to do that. This may reflect the spirit of the post-socialism too, that the minimum level of existence may also include housing. Not many would think that this should not be so (~33%) but it is also not to conclude that these people would say that prior saving is the answer to such problems[8]. One thing is clear though, that respondents do punish those, who get into trouble upon their own faults, whatever this might mean. Obviously, the divorce is such a thing, whereas getting sick, of whatever kind, is not. In any event, these results should be read cautiously. The respondents are young, without own experience of the nature of a marriage and the diseases at all.

3.2 Helping but how?

In the next scenario, this first question is endowed with a different background. The aim of the loan is different, thus the debtor, under the same circumstances, wishes to acquire a luxurious sport car or a luxurious vacation[9], instead of a flat for the family. The failure of performance is however the same. Firstly, in case of the global financial crisis, the willingness to help the debtor is (relative to the above) very low. (yes: 14.53% – no: 82.40%).

Secondly, however, when the failed performance is due to the illness of the spouse, the wanted help is higher again. (yes: 54.75% – no: 42.18%).

---

[7] Please note, that a few answer was illegible or missing, therefore the total of "yes" and "no" shall not be 100%.

[8] Quite certainly, there is no such question about savings, since otherwise the respondents would have reacted in a biased way.

[9] 'Luxury' might have meant 'greed' to some but 'necessity' to others. Assumedly, the answers reflect the distinctions

Thirdly, the vast majority refuses to help in the event of a divorce. (yes: 12.01% – no: 84.64%).

The respondents are seemingly less sympathetic with the idea of a luxurious spending financed out of a loan. However it is still robustly accepted and supported if someone fails due to illness (~ 55% would help). It seems, that illness is regarded as an utterly bad and unjust fate, no matter why and how, which must be remedied. Clearly, however the *objective* of the spending (out of loan) makes quite a difference.

3.3 What is the role of responsibility?

In the final scenario, the loan is used differently again. Instead of buying a flat or getting a luxurious car or entertainment, the aim here is to purchase further real estates as investments for the future.

If global financial crisis caused the debtor to fail the performance, a substantial majority of the respondents would say "no" to a helping request here. (yes: 24.58% – no: 72.35%).

If however the spouse's illness were the reason to stop paying back the loan, the respondents would be more willing to help. (yes: 62.29% – no: 33.52%).

In case of divorce, on the other hand, this helping willingness plummets again. (yes: 13.41% – no: 80.73%).

Interestingly enough, if one takes a closer look at the results of these three basic scenarios, it is striking what differences there are in the answers.

Table 1 Causes of failures compared

Yes for help in housing	**Yes** for help in luxurious spending	**Yes** for help in further real estate as investment	Cause of failures
63.13 %	14.53%	24.58 %	global crisis
84.64 %	54.75 %	62.29 %	illness of spouse
20.95 %	12.01 %	13.41 %	divorce

It seems to be important for the respondents what the aim of the long-term loan agreement is, and whether it is so justified, so as to be worth a common help. The minimum living existence (i.e. housing) is clearly more worth than a luxurious spending or a speculation as an investment. In any event, the respondents are also reacting on the variety of the causes of failures. The global financial crisis triggers help but much less than illness does.

It might well be the case that for these youngsters a divorce is such an overriding self default, that it is not worth further inquiries what the circumstances are/were. And it is true on the other way around, i.e. the spouse's illness is such a devastating impact that should be outweighed with help, again, regardless to the circumstances.

The questionnaire consisted of further inquiries related to the above mentioned scenarios, digging for the "why"s and the "how"s of the plain "yes" and "no" answers. The basic scenarios remaining the same, the later answers are analyzed in relation with the earlier ones. So these cross-references are supposed to show what a respondent would say for further questions if at the start he decided for yes, for helping those in financial need, or on the other way round, what a respondent would say for further questions, if at the start he decided for no, for not helping those in financial need. Therefore the tables below (Table 2-4) demonstrate also a cross reference scrutiny to the very questions, in which the first line of answers indicate whether the respondent would help (yes) or would not (no). Corollary, it means that the responses in the rows are related to the responses in the columns (yes-no).

4. The analysis

As a base line results here are the most important assessments concluded during the survey, subject to the analysis and evidences, of course, as hopefully provided below.

4.1.One can hardly distinguish among the respondents as to their attitude towards the state and the free market. Distrust in both institutions is just almost palpable.

4.2. The market rules are selectively accepted. In case of market failure the solutions are generally implicitly expected from the state.

4.3. Readiness to help others in need is relatively widespread if and only the cause is not self-inflicted and the spending is justified.

4.4. However well acknowledged it is, that market failures are indispensable, the expected cure from the state regulations are just not trusted.

4.1 One can hardly distinguish among the respondents as to their attitude towards the state (and the free market). Distrust in both institutions, market and state, is just almost palpable.

Firstly, the question is, what do the respondents think, when to help, indeed, what sort of deliberation is to be concerned in the decision-makings. (The role of private savings).

In the first question, our fictitious debtor might have been a responsible person and besides the loan, he would make some savings too. So he would take care of his own pension, private health service and future education for his children. In these cases a new question arises in all scenarios, namely, whether the respondent would reconsider his willingness or refusal to help, if he knew that the debtor could not pay because he has saved (or is just saving) money for retirement, illness and education for his children.

In the case of a global financial crisis the answers are the following (Table 2/A).

In Aa) case, i.e. when the debt is spent on a flat to live in, those who would help in the first place, would more likely reconsider their positive answer than those who would not support the debtor at all. It should be noted here, that the "yes" group formed quite the majority, i.e. 63.13% of the respondents. So it seems, that almost half (42.11%) of the respondents ready to help in need, would not assist to the debtor, if they knew, the debtor had savings (no matter what sort of savings).

Table 2 Saving for what?

<table>
<tr><td></td><td></td><td colspan="6">Minibrain has an average but well-paying job, which allows him to make plans for long-term future as well. He and his wife live with their 2 minor kids together.</td></tr>
<tr><td></td><td></td><td colspan="2">A/a) They want a bigger flat, because they still live at Minibrain's parents. So he calculated that since he cannot afford to buy a flat. he takes a loan, which he later fails to pay in due instalments, and while his flat is going to be auctioned, the rest of the debt is still to be paid back</td><td colspan="2">A/b) Minibrain wants to have a sport-car/a luxury vacation and calculates that even if he had such a solid financial background he would not be able to cover such an expense. So he takes a loan which he later fails to pay in due instalments, and while his flat is going to be auctioned, the rest of the debt is still to be paid back.</td><td colspan="2">A/c) Minibrain thinks it is a good investment to purchase further real estates, to lease them or later to sell them for more. So he takes a loan which he later fails to pay in due instalments, and while his flat is going to be auctioned, the rest of the debt is still to be paid back</td></tr>
<tr><td rowspan="4">A</td><td></td><td colspan="2">If he failed because his employer is wound up due to the global economic crisis.</td><td colspan="2">If he failed because his employer is wound up due to the global economic crisis.</td><td colspan="2">If he failed because his employer is wound up due to the global economic crisis.</td></tr>
<tr><td></td><td colspan="2">Would you help him?</td><td colspan="2">Would you help him?</td><td colspan="2">Would you help him?</td></tr>
<tr><td>answer</td><td>yes</td><td>no</td><td>yes</td><td>no</td><td>yes</td><td>no</td></tr>
<tr><td></td><td>63.13%</td><td>32.90%</td><td>14.53%</td><td>82.40%</td><td>24.58%</td><td>72.35%</td></tr>
<tr><td>Would you reconsider it, if he could not pay because he saved money for retirement, illness and education for his children?</td><td>yes</td><td>42.11%</td><td>9.20%</td><td>50.19%</td><td>1.10%</td><td>38.94%</td><td>8.51%</td></tr>
<tr><td></td><td></td><td colspan="2">If he failed because his wife got seriously ill and the treatment is expensive, time consuming and finally he looses his job too.</td><td colspan="2">If he failed because his wife got seriously ill and the treatment is expensive, time consuming and finally he looses his job too.</td><td colspan="2">If he failed because his wife got seriously ill and the treatment is expensive, time consuming and finally he looses his job too.</td></tr>
</table>

		Minibrain has an average but well-paying job, which allows him to make plans for long-term future as well. He and his wife live with their 2 minor kids together.					
		A/a) They want a bigger flat, because they still live at Minibrain's parents. So he calculated that since he cannot afford to buy a flat. he takes a loan, which he later fails to pay in due instalments, and while his flat is going to be auctioned, the rest of the debt is still to be paid back		**A/b)** Minibrain wants to have a sport-car/a luxury vacation and calculates that even if he had such a solid financial background he would not be able to cover such an expense. So he takes a loan which he later fails to pay in due instalments, and while his flat is going to be auctioned, the rest of the debt is still to be paid back.		**A/c)** Minibrain thinks it is a good investment to purchase further real estates, to lease them or later to sell them for more. So he takes a loan which he later fails to pay in due instalments, and while his flat is going to be auctioned, the rest of the debt is still to be paid back	
B		Would you help him?		Would you help him?		Would you help him?	
	answer	yes	no	yes	no	yes	no
		84.64%	11.73%	54.75%	42.18%	62.29%	33.52%
Would you reconsider it, if he could not pay because he saved money for retirement, illness and education for his children?	**yes**	44.44%	9.79%	11.79%	9.79%	34.25%	4.55%
C		If he failed because he and his wife decide to divorce and the facilitation of the two separate lives imposes significant financial burden.		If he failed because he and his wife decide to divorce and the facilitation of the two separate lives imposes significant financial burden.		If he failed because he and his wife decide to divorce and the facilitation of the two separate lives imposes significant financial burden.	
		Would you help him?		Would you help him?		Would you help him?	
	answer	yes	no	yes	no	yes	no
		20.95%	74.58%	12.01%	84.64%	13.41%	80.73%
Would you reconsider it, if he could not pay because he saved money for retirement, illness and education for his children?	**yes**	34.02%	12.10%	31.39%	8.43%	43.61%	9.99%

Seemingly, the Ab) case is not much of a difference. In Ab) case, i.e. the luxurious spending case, a little more than the half (50.19%) of the "yes" respondents would reconsider the help and would be far less sympathetic with the debtor, if he knew about the savings. Here the odds is however, that this "little more than half" relates to a much less group of the respondents, the 14.53% original "no" group (as opposed to the 63.13%). So it means, that the pattern is the same: the half of the 'yes' majority would reconsider the answer. But the multitude here is much less. These figures make difference only in relation to the total responding population. In Aa) those who would reconsider their positive answers are 25% of the respondents whereas in Ab) only 7%.

Finally, the reconsideration of the 'yes' group is the least likely in case Ac), in which investments/speculations are the target of the loan. However, the difference between Aa) and Ac) seems to be within just a margin of deviation (42.11% vs. 38.94%). But this 38.94% is counted from the 20.95% "yes" of the original help group as opposed to that of the 74.58% "no". Nevertheless, the pattern is resembling to that of Aa) and Ab).

To add it all up, one could draw the conclusion, that those who would not help in the first place at all – no matter whether they are in the majority or in the minority – would be less likely to reconsider their answers. And here, this point must be stressed even more. Because, the question could be construed the other way round, so that to emphasize that although one would not help right away, but would do so, nonetheless, upon learning that the debtor failed because he had had savings, thus the debtor proves to be a rational one, worthy of support. It seems that this kind of interpretation did not occur.

Conspicuously enough, when the failure to perform is due to the spouse's illness, the answers look very different (Table 2/B). The luxurious spending in case of the illness of the debtor's wife is the least favorable, therefore the least supportable deed among all things. The swings of reconsideration or not, i.e. the saying of "no" help instead of "yes" help, is the highest. (see Ab) in Table 2/A: 50.19%, Ab) in Table 2/B: 11.79%, and Ab) in Table 2/C.: 31.39%). Nevertheless it should be borne in mind that these figures are very little if related to the total responses: they range from ~5.5% to ~7%.

And finally, if the stoppage of pay back is owe to the divorce, the results are as expected, (relatively) in accordance with the first scenario, i.e. in the case of global financial crisis (Table 2/C.). The difference however is still, that the original "yes" groups are smaller in this case, than in the housing provision case. That should definitely mean, that this investment/ speculation is rather regarded as business or as speculation which in failure would not worth public help.

One way to think about this, is that whatever the differences there might be, these data show little respect to the reasons why someone gets into trouble other than illness or divorce in the first place. As opposed to that, the very reason, that someone does have the aim to take care of himself and also of his family, matters little. Thus one inevitably gets to the conclusion, that (financial) responsibility, (financial) autonomy, thereby freedom (of the state?) means little among young respondents.

Another way to analyze these data, and it is remaining certainly unproven here, is whether or not these reconsiderations mean that the respondents look at the situation not as a sign of responsibility, but as a sign of financial capability of the debtor to pay out his debt. This attitude may therefore be interpreted as a manner mirroring a pure market answer. No one is in need who still has savings.

However, if this speculative thinking is right, this train of thought might also reflect a kind of lack of institutional thinking (in financial matters). First of all, long-term savings may not necessarily guarantee liquidity. Second of all the bridging loans are designed also for exactly this kind of situations. Terminating a long-term savings contract before it is due, is not less of a damage than it is not to perform on time an installment of paying back a loan. If someone takes into consideration that long-term savings are delayed demands, then as a matter of social efficiency, the help in such a need should be, or may be, tackled with differently. Corollary, the discrepancy here between social justice and economic efficiency may be found to be false, but not for the respondents.

Besides it should be noted, however, that in general, it is not acceptable, as such, if someone without the means asks a loan for luxurious spending. And this remains even then so, when it turns out that the debtor had savings nonetheless.

And this is absolutely different from the case, in which sickness is involved in the failure of the performance. Certainly, this traditional view and this traditional ambience of sickness may seem anachronistic: "if you are ill, stay in bed". But, clearly, there are so many kinds of illness. Also, one should consider, that in Hungary, the health insurance is part of the state budget, however separate, and the contribution is collected as tax revenue. Illness is therefore already regarded as a living on public funds. No need for further support in case of luxurious expenses. Or it may be construed, in the contrary, that it is well justified (accepted) that ill people should be subsidized out of the public funds. But/or, corollary, people in Hungary have the impression, as a matter of fact, that ill people are generally poor or may become very quickly as one.

Briefly comparing these results for the sake of a possible conclusion, one might add the following doubts. The real question of the survey here was supposed to enquire the idea of self-support, or savings attitudes. It seems that the respondents would be more likely to help those in need who lack the means to get out of the financial problem. So far, so good. Since the here advocated help of the respondents proves to be, implicitly, state subsidized intervening measures (see below), it certainly causes some stress on the public budget, therefore this answer seems to be economically correct, efficient and pacifying. Those who have savings should use it first and then be aided by the community.

There are many distinctive and delicate ramifications of this attitude though. One is political, i.e. however this conclusion might be true, voters tend to think differently. (And this is so despite the fact that one could say the students represent rather the middle class than the lower or the lowest strata of the society or of the voters.) The other one is financial and not less complicated. If one really ponders on the original question here, it should be obvious, that these kinds of savings are not at all (or not necessarily) big monies or significant wealth. These may rather be considered as conscious behavior of the middle class civic virtue attitude, to act as a financially independent individual. An individual of its Lockean or even Kantian sense and an independence in its conception as that of the enlightenment. So perhaps confusingly enough, to conclude that precisely those should be helped who lack the possibility to survive a financial crisis at the expense of those who have made certain savings – just in order to avoid exactly this financial trap – proves to be the trick of the reason. This kind of solutions therefore may become counter-productive. There seem to be no motivation at all to act financially responsible[10]. The third one is a sociological consideration, or educational for that matter. There is no doubt that only the most vulnerable needs to be protected in case of financial need and that it should be done even through the public assistance, i.e. the public budget. And it is true as well, of course, that this help may only be carried out at the expense of those, who are not in financial trouble, or less hurt by the crisis for whatever reason. Although it is all a matter of degree too. Notwithstanding, this kind of thinking creates a political-economic circulus vitiosus, which needs to be broken. And it can be done only through education (whatever that might mean, for generations to come or learning from scratch for every generation).

Secondly, the question is, helping but how. (The role of bankruptcy or preferential tax regime). The specific questions here concern two separate issues. Both of them may qualify as measures of definite state interventions but they put the burden of losses differently on the loss bearers. One of the questions is whether the respondent would support an individual bankruptcy for the debtor, the other one is whether the respondent would support a preferential tax system for private debtors. If one accepts the idea of individual bankruptcy, i.e. supports it, however intrusive it might be into the private sphere of the contractual parties, the losses nevertheless are still to be born by the parties to the contract themselves. It is merely a new risk allocation which is being (re)negotiated in a case like this. On the other hand, if one promotes a preferential tax system for the private debtors, then he goes along with a distribution of losses among the taxpayers, which means among third parties, outsiders, to the contract.

In any event, the real question in law is whether these long-term contractual obligations are binding no matter what, or there should be certain possibilities to the parties for renegotiations. If this latter were accepted, then the exact procedure should be laid down in advance, so that business calculations were possible. As a matter of fact, in private debts, one recognizes the rules of the consumer protection laws here, providing for the room for maneuver in advance, in which

[10] This kind of arguments are also often used in the debates when the principles of the income tax regime is discussed: proportional, linear, fixed, etc. (Byrne, 1999 or Schoenblum, 1995).

the parties may (fairly) reorganize their rights and duties, such as amending the contract or terminating the contract, etc.

The individual bankruptcy however, is not the legal institute per se of the consumer protection. Since this allows, or rather facilitates, the renegotiations between the parties under strictly regulated circumstances, this is a much harsher state intervention forcing the creditors to enter into a new agreement if the private debtor unilaterally so requested. Good such law may create a win-win position however, thus it is not entirely a market unfriendly legal institution. The losses are taken by the parties themselves according to their new, certainly not quite regulation-free, agreement.

As opposed to that, the preferential tax system for private debtors, distorts the markets. One could certainly add that preferential tax system does exist in free markets as well, so to distinguish this legal institution, might be a little problematic for youngsters. Because what may fit to the business investments, may not be so for private spenders. The nature of their costs, the social costs are different, the (social) effectivity of the concluded but so failed private contracts is dubious[11]. Free market can deal with external costs if and only there is no better solution for the socially desired contractual relations, see national defense or clean air, etc. But private spending is very different and may trigger many more problems beyond reach of this survey, such as biased administrative decisions (corruption) or misrepresentation, etc.

One way of looking at the tables above (Table 3/A-3/C.), is to ask, how binding these long-term contractual obligations are to the debtors according to the respondents[12]. Not very much surprisingly, those who originally responded positively to help out those in financial need, answer overwhelmingly positive also to the questions whether they would support various state interfering measures.

If the performance failed because of the worldwide financial crisis, the majority of the respondents would support the help even with certain state intervention such as the individual bankruptcy and a little less intensively with the preferential tax regime[13]; see Aa) (Table 3/A). The pattern is somewhat similar in case of

---

[11] But of course requires concerns. No one likes homeless people lingering around.

[12] Sadly enough, the answers may be confusing (the questions might have been confusing too), especially when compared with the third/last question in the line below (see there). Since the institution of private bankruptcy was non-existent even in the public discourse until mid-2015, its conception must have been a vague and broad idea of the respondents, meaning a special kind of termination of the contractual relation from 2013 to 2015. This reflects speculation of course, supported only by teaching experiences rather than data. The students in class at the beginning can hardly distinguish a winding up or a bankruptcy, let alone a private/individual bankruptcy.

[13] Please note, that the tables (Tables 3/A-3/C.) show the "yes" in the first row and the "no" in the second row. Therefore, in the second ("no") row the opposite results are to be calculated. Albeit this might be more obscure and harder to interpret, the reason why these tables nevertheless use this sort of form is that this might reflect the first impression better, namely that those who would help, would trust the market less, therefore presumably support individual bankruptcy as opposed to the preferential tax regime. Here thus the comparison would like to rely heavily on the expectations of the state duties.

luxurious expenses, provided that one bears in mind that here the original "yes" group is the minority (14.53%); see Ab). The interesting situation is the question of investment/ speculation. As known, here the vast majority would say "no" (72.35%) and the vast majority of this (73.78%) says "no" to the preferential tax system as a measure to help in need as well; see Ac). On the other hand the support of the private bankruptcy is the highest in this group. Clearly, this scenario is regarded as business not worthy of help from public monies.

Having the above mentioned in mind, not surprisingly, this willingness to help is much much higher when the pay back was stopped due to the fact that the debtor's spouse had become ill. The exception is again the luxurious expense in case of illness (Table3/B.). It is perhaps obvious, that the average respondent puts the blame on the creditors here. Why was money lended at all? Was it for profit? The further question occurs here though, whether respondents are able to distinguish the cases where the debtor is being sick at the time of entering into the contracts from those cases of getting the serious illness later, during the time of effectivity of the contract. Distinctions like these ones, are hard to be reflected in this survey, of course, especially because the respondents are students, who are quite likely not to have personal experiences with contracts, negotiations, and more importantly with the alleged prudential activities of the creditors.

However, still there are quite a few, who believe that in case of basic housing problems for those in need the preferential tax system may be a solution, i.e. almost the half of the overwhelming majority (~44% of the 84.64% "yes" group, since 55.56% said no).

If the contract were breached because the debtor had divorced (Table 3/C.), the figures are again substantially less in favor of the debtors just as in the cases where the results reflect own faults. If help were to be granted though, there would be no significant differences whether to support the individual bankruptcy or the preferential tax regime.

All in all, the responses to the "help but how" is supposed to answer the question of how to be released from a debt, how to be free from an obligation taken upon voluntarily.

On the one hand, the responses here are in the line of the above-mentioned findings again, namely, that basically the half of those who said "yes", would not support preferential tax system, meaning, that the help should not necessarily be provided for by the state budget. These results may trigger the interpretation that the respondents may well be aware of their personal financial interests as taxpayers in not advocating a preferential tax regime for the debtors in failure.

On the other hand, the idea of individual bankruptcy, however unclear this institution for the respondents might have been, seems to be quite as popular (or unpopular) for solving the problem as the preferential tax regime is, albeit in a way this allows the debtor to be released from his duties at the expense of the creditors rather than the taxpayers.

Since individual bankruptcy is rather missing in the public discourse the respondents might have been less familiar with this, and especially with its operation and aim. As a general conclusion, it could be confirmed though, that except for the minimum existing expectations, i.e. the provision of housing to those in need, where the majority would be the most sympathetic towards the debtors, the respondents are not very much in favor of these kinds of measures, or they are quite split on it, to say the least. Thus, in brief, this would just strengthen the main characteristic result of the survey, meaning that the respondents equally lack the trust in both the state and the market solutions.

And thirdly or finally, one of the most intriguing questions, not only for lawyers, is the following one: whether the profit making is an evil per se. (The role of responsibility, and not only for bad economic decisions).

Whether it is acceptable that the market situations are not necessarily win-win positions and so if there are bad financial calculations, the outcome of the decisions needs to be borne by the decision-maker. Or quite to the contrary, whether there should be a mandatory state correction for market failures, so that to insulate decision-makers from the consequences of their own decisions.

This allows to ask whether the long-term loan agreement is to be (may be) terminated because of the problems having occurred on the debtor's side but far beyond the debtor's reach. It means that certain events, such as war, epidemy, natural disaster, global financial crisis, uprise, revolution, etc., may not be the doing of either party, still they have the almost unendurable impact on them or only one of them. Should it matter to us, if only one party suffers from the devastating affect, or if one of the party is better off, while the other is ruined owe to the changes in the circumstances, or should it not. In case of a private long-term loan agreement, there is no doubt, that the creditor undertakes a substantial risk, since the creditor generally does perform at once upon signing the contract, whereas the debtor has time to pay back. And this separation of deliveries of the parties to the contract, this discrepancy allowed by time, would make the risks of the parties unbalanced, unless specific guarantees are provided for in the terms and conditions otherwise.

But what sort of events may be excusable or foreseeable and what others not? The respondents in this survey, seemingly, decided that global financial crisis or illness are excusable, thus may trigger a rearrangement of the risk allocations. Divorce, on the other hand is not (see tables above). Now, why are they excusable? Does this mean that financial crisis and illness are unforeseeable and divorce is not? Nevertheless some would definitely say that divorce is much more foreseeable in the modern western culture than epidemy. Whereas there, certainly, are regions on earth, (even in Hungary too, nowadays) where the opposite should be true.

Table 3 Helping but how?

	Minibrain has an average but well-paying job, which allows him to make plans for long-term future as well. He and his wife live with their 2 minor kids together.						
		A/a) They want a bigger flat, because they still live at Minibrain's parents. So he calculated that since he cannot afford to buy a flat. he takes a loan, which he later fails to pay in due instalments, and while his flat is going to be auctioned, the rest of the debt is still to be paid back		**A/b)** Minibrain wants to have a sport-car/a luxury vacation and calculates that even if he had such a solid financial background he would not be able to cover such an expense. So he takes a loan which he later fails to pay in due instalments, and while his flat is going to be auctioned, the rest of the debt is still to be paid back.		**A/c)** Minibrain thinks it is a good investment to purchase further real estates, to lease them or later to sell them for more. So he takes a loan which he later fails to pay in due instalments, and while his flat is going to be auctioned, the rest of the debt is still to be paid back	
A		If he failed because his employer is wound up due to the global economic crisis.		If he failed because his employer is wound up due to the global economic crisis.		If he failed because his employer is wound up due to the global economic crisis,	
		Would you help him?		Would you help him?		Would you help him?	
	answer	yes	no	yes	no	yes	no
		63.13%	32.90%	14.53%	82.40%	24.58%	72.35%
Would you support an individual bankruptcy?	yes	55.34%	15.30%	65.96%	5.20%	48.08%	32.30%
Would you support a preferential tax system for debtors?	no	48.80%	19.70%	58.17%	7.90%	46.63%	73.78%
B		If he failed because his wife got seriously ill and the treatment is expensive, time consuming and finally he looses his job too.		If he failed because his wife got seriously ill and the treatment is expensive, time consuming and finally he looses his job too.		If he failed because his wife got seriously ill and the treatment is expensive, time consuming and finally he looses his job too.	
		Would you help him?		Would you help him?		Would you help him?	
	answer	yes	no	yes	no	yes	no
		84.64%	11.73%	54.75%	42.18%	62.29%	33.52%
Would you support an individual bankruptcy?	yes	61.81%	25.83%	16.39%	25.83%	51.57%	21.29%
Would you support a preferential tax system for debtors?	no	55.56%	81.03%	14.73%	81.03%	42.36%	84.21%

C		If he failed because he and his wife decide to divorce and the facilitation of the two separate lives imposes significant financial burden.		If he failed because he and his wife decide to divorce and the facilitation of the two separate lives imposes significant financial burden.		If he failed because he and his wife decide to divorce and the facilitation of the two separate lives imposes significant financial burden.	
		Would you help him?		Would you help him?		Would you help him?	
	answer	yes	no	yes	no	yes	no
		20.95%	74.58%	12.01%	84.64%	13.41%	80.73%
Would you support an individual bankruptcy?	yes	52.05%	31.50%	50.65%	29.22%	49.62%	26.97%
Would you support a preferential tax system for debtors?	no	59.02%	74.82%	44.82%	79.22%	49.62%	79.15%

Here are the results for the case of failure to perform in global financial crisis (Table 4/A). It shows clearly, that the majority would help in need (63.13%) and the overwhelming majority of these respondents who say "yes" to the help, would not agree with an interpretation that the creditors are profiteers. Therefore, only the 7% of all respondents would say the contracts are not to be paid back. So, implicitly, they do not seriously mean that the contracts should not be fulfilled.

But who should have the burden of failure then? Notwithstanding, if one looks at the other figures of the "no" group (32.9%), here the overwhelming majority is more inclined to blame the creditors (only 28.3% says no), and probably let the parties negotiate (see Aa) in Table 4/A) But these figures are also miniscule, i.e. 7% of all respondents. In case of the luxurious expenses the respondents have not too much of the solidarity. 82.40% would not help in the economic crisis for these spendings but would implicitly blame the creditors. Although only 9.80% of the 82.40% (these are the "no"-s) of these "no" respondents would say that the creditors are not usurers and the contractual obligations should be fulfilled, but this is 7% of the total answerers again.

But who are the creditors? Banks, financial institutions, friends or employers, state, perhaps? And when are they the creditors? After having helped out a debtor in need with a bridging loan in a financial global crisis?

This is fairly different in the case, in which the failure to perform is due to the wife's illness and the spending out of loan covered luxurious entertainments (Table 4/B).

Here it seems to be obvious that the majority would feel solidarity for ill people, but would not support a luxurious expense, if someone is ill. In fact, this has been the case above (and here, see Table 4/C) too if one looks at the figures of luxurious expenses being cross referenced with the illness of the debtor's wife. Nevertheless, here it is more conspicuous than anywhere else, but for the above table (Table 4/C), that it is not at all clear whether the respondents believe, the creditors should have the burden of risk. In conjunction with what was said above about the attitude towards the problems of deseases though, the respondents here hold the creditors more liable for lending money irrationally, or lending rather for profiteering.

This interpretation raises further legally more relevant questions: when should an event be foreseeable for which one has to take the liability in a contractual relation. In case of a long-term loan agreement, the answer should clearly be that right at the entering into the contract.

The reason for this is the elapse of time between the exchange of performances of the contractual parties (Csehi, 2015)[14]. Thus sickness may only be foreseeable if the circumstances in the given case so suggest. Seemingly, the respondents here think, that the probability of a serious sickness is higher than that of the (global) financial crisis or of the divorce, as a matter of fact. Therefore the creditor bears the risk for sickness, since the creditor should have known it better and/or calculated it.

Even if it were true that the Hungarian people are generally sick, it should also be a common sense knowledge, that in every 20 years of an investment or a loan agreement or whatever, there will be at least 5-7 bad years too.

Perhaps, of course, it can also be construed, that the case of the divorce is not that it is unforeseeable[15], but that it is own fault (Table 4/C). The figures in this divorce case are again different, but certainly in comfort with the other answers in the previous cases (Table 3/C.), where the pay back is stopped by the divorce of the debtor.

As an average, the respondents feel like helping is necessary for the failing debtors, unless the debtors' situation can be attributed to their own fault, such as divorce. This exception of divorce may however derive from the young and idealistic age of the respondents rather than represents a social exclusion.

[14] This foreseeability and the damages problems may certainly be different if the contract is about management services (Csehi, 2015).

[15] According to the statistics (KSH, 2013.), in the last three decades the numbers of the divorces in Hungary were the following: 1990: 24.888, 2000: 23.987, 2012: 21.830, 2013: 20.000 (estimate) and the number of the marriages: 1990: 66.405, 2000: 48.110, 2012: 36.161, 2013: 36.900 (estimate). Clearly half as many got married as got divorced. This cannot be construed as unforeseeable but surely still as self-default.

4.2 The market rules are selectively accepted, in case of market failure the solutions are generally implicitly expected from the state.

The processed data in the tables above (Tables 1-3) have further implications. The answers design a relatively ambiguous pattern about whether an obligation needs to be performed in the long run and who is to bear the burden of failure. Notwithstanding that the vast majority of the respondents accept that the creditors (banks?) are not profiteers or usurers as seen in tables above (Tables 3/A-3/C.), yet, only a few of them would go along with the consequences of such a decision. This straightforward conclusion however needs some clarifications and distinctions, of course.

Albeit depending on the situation, the majority would be willing to help in the case of the basic housing problems even if the overwhelming majority of these respondents would not necessarily blame the creditors for such circumstances. In these scenarios the "no" help groups are in minority and basically these are the most anxious about the creditors' being profiteers and would allow the non-performance of these contracts from the part of the debtors (see explicitly Table 4/A). One might realize right away, that these are the scenarios, where failure of the performance is caused by the global economic crisis. Therefore clearly, here the respondents blame the creditors for the surrounding problems. necessarily blame the creditors for such circumstances.

The first explanation would be that the respondents simply do not care. They accept that help is needed, meaning also that they would expect to be assisted in such a case, but they do not bother further. This could also reflect that solidarity might well be in their thinking but not in their acting. Therefore implicitly, all these answers boil down to an acceptance or expectation of state interventions. They have no better idea. They do not trust the state but neither the market solutions.

Another possible interpretation may be that the vast majority believes that the contracts should be fulfilled and if impossibility occurs then it is not termination, but rather a possible modification of the contract is needed. And for this, rules are needed, of course. Market rules or state regulations? The first would lead to a circle problem, the latter to the state intervention again, implicitly.

In any event, these possible clarifications do not exclude each other. In the end, both conclusions come to the inevitable reliance in the state measures, even if only implicitly. Those respondents who would be willing to help right away incline to imply to a state measure of intervention into the market affairs. No further enquiry is needed, it is the task of the state to manage somehow. The big split in answering to the method of help (Tables 2/A-2/C) demonstrates the uncertainty of the respondents in this matter.

Table 4 Whether the profit-making is an evil *per se*? What is the role of responsibility?

	Minibrain has an average but well-paying job, which allows him to make plans for long-term future as well. He and his wife live with their 2 minor kids together.						
		A/a) They want a bigger flat, because they still live at Minibrain's parents. So he calculated that since he cannot afford to buy a flat. he takes a loan, which he later fails to pay in due instalments, and while his flat is going to be auctioned, the rest of the debt is still to be paid back		**A/b)** Minibrain wants to have a sport-car/a luxury vacation and calculates that even if he had such a solid financial background he would not be able to cover such an expense. So he takes a loan which he later fails to pay in due instalments, and while his flat is going to be auctioned, the rest of the debt is still to be paid back.		**A/c)** Minibrain thinks it is a good investment to purchase further real estates, to lease them or later to sell them for more. So he takes a loan which he later fails to pay in due instalments, and while his flat is going to be auctioned, the rest of the debt is still to be paid back	
A		If he failed because his employer is wound up due to the global economic crisis.		If he failed because his employer is wound up due to the global economic crisis.		If he failed because his employer is wound up due to the global economic crisis,	
		Would you help him?		Would you help him?		Would you help him?	
	answer	yes	no	yes	no	yes	no
		63.13%	32.90%	14.53%	82.40%	24.58%	72.35%
Many believe that creditors are rich and usurers (profiteers), therefore in these cases the pay back is not obligatory. And you?	no	83.73%	28.30%	99.80%	9.80%	80.29%	86.62%
B		If he failed because his wife got seriously ill and the treatment is expensive, time consuming and finally he looses his job too.		If he failed because his wife got seriously ill and the treatment is expensive, time consuming and finally he looses his job too.		If he failed because his wife got seriously ill and the treatment is expensive, time consuming and finally he looses his job too.	
		Would you help him?		Would you help him?		Would you help him?	
	answer	yes	no	yes	no	yes	no
		84.64%	11.73%	54.75%	42.18%	62.29%	33.52%
Many believe that creditors are rich and usurers (profiteers), therefore in these cases the pay back is not obligatory. And you?	no	82.64%	85.80%	21.92%	85.80%	83.61%	88.04%

C		If he failed because he and his wife decide to divorce and the facilitation of the two separate lives imposes significant financial burden.		If he failed because he and his wife decide to divorce and the facilitation of the two separate lives imposes significant financial burden.		If he failed because he and his wife decide to divorce and the facilitation of the two separate lives imposes significant financial burden.	
		Would you help him?		Would you help him?		Would you help him?	
	answer	yes	no	yes	no	yes	no
		20.95%	74.58%	12.01%	84.64%	13.41%	80.73%
Many believe that creditors are rich and usurers (profiteers), therefore in these cases the pay back is not obligatory. And you?	no	82.79%	88.47%	82.04%	87.65%	78.95%	87.89%

In the introductory part of the questionnaire, there are some general questions posed to map up the respondents' financial and social backgrounds. The vast majority of the respondents live in a highly indebted environment as debtors. 75.7% of the respondents said "yes" to the question, if he was aware of any loan taken in the family.

Their mostly negative experience of getting indebted is shown in their answers to the question "to whom would they refer to in case of need for a bridging loan". In case of need the vast majority of them would rather refer to the state first and then to the parents, way ahead of a financial institute (Table 5)[16].

Table 5 Who should help you?

In case you needed a bridging loan. whom would you refer to?		
friend	**parent**	**colleague**
6.10%	26.70%	8.90%
employer	**state**	**other**
1.70%	38.60%	59.70%
	financial institute	
	8.90%	

If one considers that the informal financial help (parent) includes also that of the friends and colleagues, this figure basically equals with that of the state. This mirrors well the attitude of the respondents documented in the comments of the answers, namely that in need they would refer privately to friends and parents, because if a serious trouble occurred, they would not necessarily be expected to

16 It should be noted, that several answers were allowed to be made here.

pay back the full loan. Certainly, it must be added that these respondents are young.

The serious distrust in the state comes into this picture here too. The loan agreement if concluded with the state is less likely to be enforced, than if it were signed with a financial institution (let alone a private one[17]). The respondents obviously rely on the vision that in case of financial troubles, one would be able to (re)negotiate with the state (whatever this institution means here for them) just as one could do that with the relatives or friends.

So the question "who is the creditor" may not be irrelevant at all. Therefore special attention should be paid to the answers of the category "other"s. Most of the respondents (59.70%) would ask money from "other" than friend, parent, colleague, financial institute, employer or state.

It is striking, that in the event of financial difficulties, these youngsters would rather avoid the financial institutes. Clearly, the mistrust in the banks and other financial institutions is palpable among these respondents. This seems to be the culture: the hope (in category "others") for lottery, for a rich uncle abroad, just like in the economically weak Hungary in the beginning of the 20th c. (the Horthy-regime).

This means that these respondents grew up in an environment that tolerates the non-payback, the failure to perform, therefore rather negotiates with those whom they believe they can fail later with possibly no consequences at all (friends and parents) or with less painful consequences (state as opposed to the financial institutions).

Thus conclusively the distrust against the market solutions cannot be worse than against that of the state. Who could trust a state that can renegotiate contracts. When? Under whose mandate? And at whose expense?

Again, this attitude would lead to a sly, 'common sense' behaviour, that one should rather be indebted to the state than not at all, since if not, then he should only be net contributor to the public budget. Whatever simplistic idea this might sound this thinking may be mirrored in the answers in the survey.

It should be noted however, that these responses and comments included also, that in case they were to be asked to lend money to a friend in need, mostly they would not have asked any security for repayment either, again acknowledging the possibility of failure to perform.

[17] The arguments here necessary lead too far to the free market concept or state aid, or of the state as a market participant in the private market, etc, which cannot be discussed here.

4.3 Readiness to help others in need is relatively widespread if and only the cause is not self-inflicted and the spending is justified

Looking at the figures and the tables, one has to bear two things in mind. One would be the problem of impossibility to perform, and the other the foreseeability of this risk.

The fact that the impossibility of certain performance could be used as an excuse for the breach of a contract is not at all self-evident (Byrd, 2010). The construing of impossibility as a defense when non-performance is the fault of none of the parties, may qualify as a legal development. Instead of selling the defaulted party as a slave, he can be released from his duties. This changes in construing matters of impossibility is regarded as a legal development of bona fides in Roman Law and of Treu und Glauben (guter Glaube), good faith, fairness or equity in the various legal orders in the 18th and 19th centuries respectively (Földi, 2001).

Notwithstanding the above, the real practical question here is how to solve the problem of an inefficient private loan agreement. And in addition to it, how to solve this problem if this inefficiency is widespread in the economy and affects a great deal of average people, as the data of the survey demonstrates it well (4.2. above).

No doubt that in such market failures a state intervention has already been approved in many modern constitutionalism, especially in those of the welfare states and so in the EU[18]. Legislations, state initiated rules, introduced on behalf of those less able to create a bargaining position in free markets are not brand new, even if they become more and more nuanced (or bureaucratic?) and sometimes less sometimes more intrusive, such as the labour contracts, the consumer protection provisions or the consumer credit protection regulations, let alone the special self-governing rules or ethical codes of certain businesses.

And exactly that is why it is interesting that the respondents of this questionnaire seem to have mistrust in the state regulations almost equally to that of the market solutions, even then when they mostly believe that help is to be granted. Those who do not answer "yes" to help do not bother much. But they are in the minority.

[18] See e.g. the latest jurisdiction of the CJEU relating to the long-term (loan) agreements (C-96/14, C-449/13, C-482/13, C-484/13, C-485/13, C-487/13, etc).

4.4 However well acknowledged it is, that market failures are indispensable, the expected cure from the state regulations are just not trusted.

Besides the private debt issues, the survey was intended to spread out to the business debts and loans too.

The playing field here is designed rather for the smaller companies (SMEs). In this fictitious case again, the owner of a company has an own patent and an excellent long-term business model. Although the company had it well for a while, still, due to a decreasing demand, the turn over of the company was plummeting and turned into a loss. The owner takes more andmore loans but without further investments the company faces bankruptcy. Since the firm's assets is subject to a secured loan taken before, the company cannot receive further commercial credit or only at an extra price.

In this case the questions focused on the rules of being able to get a loan, on the administrative restrictions, if any, and on the responsibility (or even liability) of a company making solid business decisions or on the responsibility of the state to watch over these problems, if not more (see Table 6/A-6/C).

The majority of the respondents (71.2%) would not claim that the problems of the SMEs here are caused by the administrative rules. This may be interpreted in two ways though. One is that the majority accepts the market rule. The manager made bad business decisions. The other one is that the majority accepts the administrative rules as a fact but simply thinks that here this was not the cause. This is not to wonder. The question of course is always a matter of degree.

What is more telling here however (Table 6/A.), is that this group of majority which does accept the need for regulations and does not blame the administrative prescriptions would nevertheless incline to believe that one needs to lie ("declare non-realistic statements") in formal loan requests (30.50%), which is ~21% of all responses. Truly though, they are in the minority, but what a minority! Truly, also 62.90% of them (which is ~ 43% of all responses) believe that not disclosing a relevant fact in such a request form means fraud and one should be liable for that. But that is barely more than the half of the majority who accepts the rules, and not even the half of all answerers.

Now, those who do complain about the administrative rules are even more interesting. Evidently this is a tiny little group (of about 70 respondents) but are more convinced that the rules might require false statements to make (44.52%) and they also think, that this should qualify as a lie and be punished (49.57%). What kind of attitude should there be expected here if someone is determined to carry out a transparent but successful business?

And finally if one looks at the last question, it is obvious that the overwhelming majority of the respondents accept the market rules by claiming that the business decision of the manager was not adequate. So the overwhelming majority accepts the market rules but not the solution.

Table 6 Business plans, market failures and the credit

<table>
<tr><td colspan="4">Megabrain has an own patent and an excellent long-term business model. Thus his small garage-firm leases the seat and the two cars of the company. The company had made good profit for some years but recently, due to the decreasing demand, the income of the company was plummeting and turned into a loss in the last couple of years. Although there is quite a competition in the market, Megabrain manages to obtain a bridging loan from a bank owe to his good will and connections. However Megabrain does not disclose that his patent rights are going to expire and he has no intention to extend it. Without further investments, the company apparently goes bankrupt. Since the firm's assets is subject to a secured loan taken before, the company cannot receive other commercial credit or only at an extra price. In this case</td></tr>
<tr><td colspan="2" rowspan="2">A</td><td>Many would blame the rules, claiming that they set administrative obstacles for the small entrepreneurs. And You?</td><td>Many would blame the rules, claiming that they set administrative obstacles for the small entrepreneurs. And You?</td></tr>
<tr><td>yes (21.6%) in total population</td><td>no (71.2%) in total population</td></tr>
<tr><td>Many believe that debtors in a loan agreement often feel compelled to declare non-realistic statements. And You?</td><td>yes</td><td>44.52%</td><td>30.50%</td></tr>
<tr><td>Many believe that Megabrain should be liable for fraud. And You?</td><td>yes</td><td>49.57%</td><td>62.90%</td></tr>
<tr><td>Many believe that Megabrain had happened to be lucky and that lately made series of bad business decisions, and that he should have either left the business earlier or should have invested more by working harder and introducing new developments. And you?</td><td>yes</td><td>84.90%</td><td>84.10%</td></tr>
<tr><td colspan="2" rowspan="2">B</td><td>Many would blame the rules, claiming that they set administrative obstacles for the small entrepreneurs. And You?</td><td>Many would blame the rules, claiming that they set administrative obstacles for the small entrepreneurs. And You?</td></tr>
<tr><td>yes (21.6%) in total population</td><td>no (71.2%) in total population</td></tr>
<tr><td>Many believe that it is the state that has the duty to take care of small entrepreneurs in need. And You?</td><td>yes</td><td>76.65%</td><td>51.36%</td></tr>
<tr><td>tax allowance</td><td>yes</td><td>57.37%</td><td>31.52%</td></tr>
<tr><td>non-refundable support</td><td>yes</td><td>29.37%</td><td>13.23%</td></tr>
<tr><td>appointment of state liquidator</td><td>yes</td><td>11.47%</td><td>11.28%</td></tr>
<tr><td>buy out</td><td>yes</td><td>5.05%</td><td>7.00%</td></tr>
<tr><td colspan="2" rowspan="2">C</td><td>Many would blame the rules, claiming that they set administrative obstacles for the small entrepreneurs. And You?</td><td>Many would blame the rules, claiming that they set administrative obstacles for the small entrepreneurs. And You?</td></tr>
<tr><td>yes (21.6%) in total population</td><td>no (71.2%) in total population</td></tr>
<tr><td>Should there be an insurance fund financed by the market participants (companies), which in return, in case of bankruptcy, may grant favourable credit to the members/companies. And You?</td><td>yes</td><td>72.52%</td><td>56.21%</td></tr>
<tr><td>No need at all, it is the very task of the state. And You?</td><td>yes</td><td>8.27%</td><td>4.18%</td></tr>
</table>

It is just conspicuous, how the majority of the respondents, regardless whether they trust the regulations or not, expect the state most of all, implicitly or not, to manage the regulations of the business. No doubt that the acceptance of a kind of a state duty to take care of small and medium entrepreneurs is more widespread among the respondents than not (Table 6/B)[19]. And surprisingly enough (or not?), it is less so (51.36%) among those who are less suspicious about the administrative restrictions (71.2%). One way to look at it is that those who do blame the administrative obstacles in SMEs business expect more help and are more critical towards the existing rules. Thus in this case one might ponder a little bit whether the distinction between the two groups are a sign of different attitude towards the market and the state or rather it is the critical attitude towards a well rooted culture biased to state intervention which divides the "yes" and "no" groups.

This thinking might be tested in the responses of the "how". Should the state provide for tax allowance or state aid or manage more administrative intervening measures such as the appointment of state liquidator or carry out a buy-out. None of these may be considered as more market-friendly than the others, in the end all of these measures result in the taxpayers' help.

This is why it is more than striking to have a look at the answers in Table 6/C. When there is a rather market like solution of a saving management (sort of insurance, but obligatory) for a possible bankruptcy, the embracement of this institution is quite broad as opposed to that of a strict state aid (no matter what that might really mean).

5. Who shall have the burden then?

All in all, one needs to come to the conclusion from the answers above that the majority of the respondents favors implicitly the state solutions as opposed to the market one, but trusts none of them.

No doubt that the overwhelming majority of the respondents accepts the market rules but not the solutions. Or rather, they accept the advantages of the market economy but refuse to live with their disadvantages. This is no wonder.

The question is whom to put the burden of remedying the bad individual decisions, when the pushing away of the responsibility is quite widespread. This question is even more interesting if one considers the fate of windfalls. Undoubtedly, if any windfall derived from this kind of decisions benefited the debtors but not the creditors, would be awarded to the debtors right away with no hesitation at all, as it was the case before the global crisis in the so called long-term consumer loan agreements based on the foreign exchange rates.

As mentioned at the very beginning, and as is often obvious in the answers, the respondents compose a new generation in the sense, that they were born

19 Please note, that here more answers were possible

after the Transition. This generation grew up in the stumbling first steps of the democracy and the market operations. This generation is uniquely overburdened with private debt, most of which will never be paid back.

This also reflects the fact that in the childhood of these respondents (from the 1990s to the early 2000s) there were no solid foundations for a healthy financial understanding in a fast growing globalization. After having spent several decades in a command economy, then a little bit looser state-steered economy, Hungary has joined the free market economies in a time of a decreasing inflation, overall optimism about the capitalistic future, and in a swiftly growing world wide consumption. As opposed to this global economic background the country had faced serious structural economic crisis (pension, health care, education), long term financial problems, budgetary restrictions, several austerity packages without real solutions.

5.1 The minimum living existence as a fundamental (constitutional) right

The lack of private housing for youngsters has ever been a problem of the Kadar-regime, thus during (and after) the Transition this was one of the issue number one in politics too. The then newly established Constitutional Court has inherited already cases from its legal ancestor of the previous regime, dealing with the then long-term loan agreements. The issue was how to adapt the state subsidized (socialist) loan agreements to the market environment[20].

And this want of an own housing behavior, this culturally overestimated precious goods, is reflected well in the manner of the young generation too. Housing is always more supported by the respondents than not (first column in Table 7/A), in case of illness this solidarity even grows (second column in Table 7/A), but plummets considerably if they think the default was self-inflicted, as for example in the case of a divorce (third column in Table 7/A).

[20] See the constitutional Court case No. 32/1991. (VI. 6.) ABH. The case in question was about the enormous economic and financial discrepancy in the terms and conditions provided for in the newly entered long-term loan agreements on the one hand and those concluded still in the socialist regime on the other hand. The interest rate on the old loan was close to none, whereas it was around 30-35% in the new loan agreements. The legal issue here was, as is now too, whether it is justified for the state to intervene into private agreements and enforce amendments by legislation against even the wills of the (both) parties. The very circumstances differ though in a great deal, since the Transition back then had proved to be unforeseeable for the parties at the conclusion of their contracts, but never again this argument was ever accepted by the Constitutional Court until now. The article 226.§ (2) of the Civil Code of 1959 then in effect was even found by a judge back then constitutionally dubious, as a matter of fact, which however granted the means necessary for the transition to a market economy.

5.2 The luxurious expenses at the expense of others

The issue of luxurious expenses financed out of a long-term loan is a lot more complicated. Here the statements and actions do not seem to be in harmony with each other.

One way to look at it is that the negative impact of the circumstances triggers always sympathy. And it is true for quite a wild range of issues, it may be financial (economic crisis), biological (illness) or sociological (divorce) problem as certainly evidenced in the table below (Table 7/B).

Table 7 Who should have the burden of failure?

		Minibrain has an average but well-paying job, which allows him to make plans for long-term future as well. He and his wife live with their 2 minor kids together.					
		A/a) They want a bigger flat, because they still live at Minibrain's parents. So he calculated that since he cannot afford to buy a flat. he takes a loan, which he later fails to pay in due instalments, and while his flat is going to be auctioned, the rest of the debt is still to be paid back.		**A/b)** Minibrain wants to have a sport-car/a luxury vacation and calculates that even if he had such a solid financial background he would not be able to cover such an expense. So he takes a loan which he later fails to pay in due instalments, and while his flat is going to be auctioned, the rest of the debt is still to be paid back.		**A/c)** Minibrain thinks it is a good investment to purchase further real estates, to lease them or later to sell them for more. So he takes a loan which he later fails to pay in due instalments, and while his flat is going to be auctioned, the rest of the debt is still to be paid back.	
A		If he failed because his employer is wound up due to the global economic crisis.		If he failed because his employer is wound up due to the global economic crisis.		If he failed because his employer is wound up due to the global economic crisis,	
		Would you help him?		Would you help him?		Would you help him?	
answer		yes	no	yes	no	yes	no
		63.13%	32.90%	84.64%	11.73%	20.96%	74.58%
Would you reconsider it, if you knew that he could not pay because he saved money for retirement, illness and education for his children?	yes	42.11%	9.20%	44.44%	9.79%	34.02%	12.10%
Would you support an individual bankruptcy?	yes	55.34%	15.30%	61.81%	25.83%	52.05%	31.50%
Would you support a preferential tax system for debtors?	no	48.80%	19.70%	55.56%	81.03%	59.02%	74.82%
Many believe that creditors are rich and usurers (profiteers), therefore in these cases the pay back is not obligatory. And you?	no	83.73%	28.30%	82.64%	85.80%	82.79%	88.47%

B		**A/b)** Minibrain wants to have a sport-car/a luxury vacation and calculates that even if he had such a solid financial background he would not be able to cover such an expense. So he takes a loan which he later fails to pay in due instalments, and while his flat is going to be auctioned, the rest of the debt is still to be paid back.					
		Would you help him?		Would you help him?		Would you help him?	
answer		yes	no	yes	no	yes	no
		14.53%	82.40%	54.75%	42.18%	12.01%	84.64%
Would you reconsider it, if you knew that he could not pay because he saved money for retirement, ill-ness and education for his children?	yes	50.19%	1.10%	11.79%	9.79%	31.39%	8.43%
Would you support an individual bankruptcy?	yes	65.96%	5.20%	16.39%	25.83%	50.65%	29.22%
Would you support a preferential tax system for debtors?	no	58.17%	7.90%	14.73%	81.03%	44.82%	79.22%
Many believe that creditors are rich and usurers (profiteers), therefore in these cases the pay back is not obligatory. And you?	no	99.80%	9.80%	21.92%	85.80%	82.04%	87.65%

C		**A/c)** Minibrain thinks it is a good investment to purchase further real estates, to lease them or later to sell them for more. So he takes a loan which he later fails to pay in due instal-ments, and while his flat is going to be auctioned, the rest of the debt is still to be paid back					
		Would you help him?		Would you help him?		Would you help him?	
answer		yes	no	yes	no	yes	no
		24.58%	72.35%	62.29%	33.52%	13.41%	80.73%
Would you reconsider it, if you knew that he could not pay because he saved money for retirement, ill-ness and education for his children?	yes	82.79%	88.47%	82.04%	87.65%	78.95%	9.99%
Would you support an individual bankruptcy?	yes	48.08%	32.30%	51.57%	21.29%	49.62%	26.97%
Would you support a preferential tax sys-tem for debtors?	no	46.63%	73.78%	42.36%	84.21%	49.62%	79.15%
Many believe that creditors are rich and usurers (profiteers), therefore in these cases the pay back is not obligatory. And you?	no	80.29%	86.62%	83.61%	88.04%	78.95%	87.89%

Why would someone justify a common solidarity for an irrational use of others money (i.e. loan)? If one considers the cultural and historical background one is compelled to see a pattern. The desire to act and live like a rich man even at the expense of others is well rooted in the history. Truly, the vast majority would not support this idea.

However, looking at the first column, at the responses in the case of "no"s, it is striking how definitely – almost in consent – the blame is put on the creditors if the trouble was caused by the financial crisis. This means, that this young generation overwhelmingly holds the creditors (most likely the fiancial sectors in this case) responsible for the global economic crisis, and the debtors of such contracts as victims. Therefore the obligations may be forgiven. And what is more, probably that is why, it is here where the preferential tax regime is the most advocated.

And if it is so, which is very much evidenced here, the question is, those who would help (and do not think that the obligations are to be forgiven, see second column group "yes") would do that for what reason? As a matter of fact, this proves to be the group of people with real sympathy to others problems. The proper means for help is not clear though. The group is divided in almost all measures by half and half.

Further interesting results are in the third column of Table 7/B. Here, it seems, the respondents regard the speculator/investor as being part of the problem rather than a victim. So the help is missing here the most.

5.3 Speculation or investment (business without the legal formalities)

Originally, this question is to analyze the attitude towards hustlers, slickers ("ügyeskedők"). In this situation the debtor, without setting up a proper business as required by the law, acts as a "businessman" and uses the possibility to make money in a much friendlier, easier environment, clearly at the expense of others.

No doubt, this hustler manner is fairly well scattered in the Hungarian society, nevertheless the respondents do not quite seem to realise it. Unquestionably, most of them would categorize this situation as a speculation not worthy of help and as a problem caused by own fault, and the debtor himself as the problem maker rather than the victim.

This doubt of presumption however, whether here the respondents are biased against business or speculation as such or just really identified the actors as hustlers, thereby not worthy of help, remains still to be developed.

6. Conclusions

As for a really brief conclusion of the survey, one could say that the respondents act very logically and calculate very rationally. They do so, even if they mostly have no basic knowledge of the issues above but a hunch. The problem is that acting irresponsibly is rational because it pays off better than acting by the rules. To be able to embrace the disadvantages of the market economy one needs to be able to understand and manage them institutionally. This survey, as it stands now, demonstrates exactly the lack of such an insight.

The results depict a latently, vaguely rather messianistic, though not trusted, expectation from the state, whatever that should mean. This vague expectation for a solution may certainly be interpreted also as a general need to push the responsibility away. This suggestion may well be demonstrated by the answers, which show a relatively ready help but also a split mostly in half and half in the "how"s. The "how" is just does not matter. So it might reflect just a general desire of goodness without the thorough understanding of or deliberations of the (unintended) consequences[21].

Clearly these youngsters have no experiences of themselves so far, so the responses mirror rather a cultural heritage[22].

In these circumstances loan is an alternative, but exactly in these circumstances this loan is a very expensive alternative. Without trust (and it means here saving/ investment too) in the system, the price of the loan is just going to be soaring, because it may be excused to fail the agreement regardless the consequences.

As to a final impression and conclusion, one faces a very blurred picture. Albeit it is clear that the overwhelming majority of the respondents accepts that the long-term promises are binding, still quite many of them are ready to appreciate the troubles of the debtor, especially if those troubles were caused by the global economic crisis or illness. None of these causes are considered by the respondents as a risk which needs to be (or should be) calculated or managed privately right before the entering into a contract. Thus it seems that the majority of the respondents feel deeper for those in – not self-inflicted – needs. What own fault means however is not very clear and distinctive. This sympathy is also clouded by the fact that the solutions in these situations are not consequential. Their desire to help therefore are not supported by the reality but by some vague expectations from the public funds, the public hand (paraphrasing Smith).

---

21 The eagerness to insulate the decision-makers from the negative consequences of their own bad economic decisions is so vivid, that it is quite a topic again in the public discourse relating to the amendments of the brand new Civil Code. See Article. 2. of the bill No. T/10528 of the government concerning Article 3:24. on the liability of the company management in various cases.

22 This lack of trust in the state operation is surveyed – among others – by András Sajó (Sajó, 2008).

So, as it seems, the operation of the market is widely approved, working for profit is not at all cursed, provided, there are no failures. If market failure occurred, the solution is not expected from the market but rather from a vague conception of the state aid.

One might think right away, that basically this is what one witnesses also in the developed, welfare states too. In case of market failure the regulation is felt to be necessary and right. The difference is however, that here there is a traditional misgiving about the governmental interferences or reactions. Not because of the fear from the state intervening into the private autonomy, but because the state proves to be incompetent.

Assuming that these conclusions are justified, the results are quite thought-provoking. A quarter of a century after the Transition, the new generation's reactions to the occuring financial-social problems have roots in the past socialism rather than in the capitalism. The reasons why the Transition – due to the global collapse of the Soviet regime – was so distrust in a paternalistic state, the devastating experiences of state intrusion, the dislike of socialist "Gleichschaltung", the desire to motivate creativity so that to enhance individual indeundeniably overwhelmingly popular are just gone. The deep pendence, autonomy and self-esteem are not even traceable. What is left nowadays is the capitalistic objectives (an avidity to be wealthy) without the capitalistic virtues (the autonomous, financially independent, deliberating citizen).

References

1. Byrd, S. B. (2010). *Einführung in die Anglo-Amerikanische Rechtssprache* (Introduction to Anglo-American Law and Language) Band II/Vol II. Contracts and Torts. 2. Auflage. p.371. C.H.Beck –Stämpfli. (in German)
2. Byrne, D. M. (1999). Locke, Property and Progressive Taxes. *Nebraska Law Review.* 78(3), pp. 700-738.
3. Csehi, Z. (2015). A vezető tisztségviselő polgári jogi felelősségének alapjai és irányai az új Polgári Törvénykönyv alapján. (Legal Foundations and Trends of Civil Law Liability of the Chief Executive Officer according to the new Civil Code.), In: Csehi, Z., Szabó, M. (eds.) *A vezető tisztségviselő felelőssége.* (*Liability of the Chief Executive Officer.*) (pp. 9-50.) CompLex Wolters Kluwer, Budapest. (in Hungarian)
4. Fleck, Z., Gajduschek, Gy. (2015). Empirikus kutatás a jogban. (Empirical Research in Law.) In: Jakab, A., Menyhárd, A. (eds.) *A jog tudománya*: Tudománytörténeti és tudományelméleti írások, gyakorlati tanácsokkal. (Jurisprudence.) (pp. 101-131.) HVG-ORAC Lap- és Könyvkiadó Kft. (in Hungarian)
5. Földi, A. (2001). A jóhiszeműség és tisztesség elve. Intézménytörténeti vázlat a római jogtól napjainkig. (The Principle of Bona Fidei. A Historical-institutional Outline from the Roman Law upto Now.) ELTE Állam- és Jogtudományi Kar, Budapest. (in Hungarian)

6. Földi, A. (2004). *A másért való felelősség a római jogban, jogelméleti és összehasonlító polgári jogi kitekintéssel.* (Liability for Others in Roman Law.) Rejtjel, Budapest. (in Hungarian)
7. Griffiths, M. R., Lucas, J. R. (1996). Ethical Economics. Palgrave-MacMillan.
8. Hatzis, A. N. (2015). Moral Externalities: An Economic Approach to the Legal Enforcement of Morality. In: Hatzis, A. N., Mercuro, N. (eds.) Law and Economics: Philosophical Issues and Fundamental Questions. (pp. 226- 244.) Routledge, London/New York. [Online]. Available from: http:// ssrn.com/abstract=2821292 [Accessed: 23rd August 2016.]
9. KSH (2013). Statisztikai Tükör. (Statistical Mirror.) Népmozgalom. (People's movement.) Budapest. (in Hungarian)
10. Pázmándi, K. (2015). A nyelvvel való visszaélés rétegei a pénzpiacokkal kapcsolatos kereskedelmi és politikai kommunikációban. (Layers of abusing language in commercial and political communications related to the money-markets). In: Szabó, M. (ed.) A jog nyelvi dimenziója. (Dimension of the Language of Law.) (pp. 257-266.) Bíbor Kiadó, Miskolc. (in Hungarian)
11. Picketty, T. (2015). Economy of Inequality. Harvard University Press
12. Picketty, T. (2014). The Capital in the 21st Century. Harvard University Press.
13. Sajó, A. (2008). Az állam működési zavarainak társadalmi újratermelése. (Social reproduction of state operating functions). Közgazdasági Szemle. 55(7-8), pp. 690-711. (in Hungarian)
14. Schoenblum, J. (1995). Tax fairness or unfairness? A consideration of the philosophical bases for unequal taxation of individuals. The American Journal of Tax Policy. 12, pp. 221-271.

Chapter 2.

RISKS OF NON-DEVIATION FROM THE ABSOLUTE PRIORITY RULE IN BANKRUPTCY CASES[23]

This chapter is about bankruptcies in SMEs. The assets of an ailing company are to be divided differently among the various classes of creditors if it is decided in a reorganization or in a liquidation procedure. During liquidation it is the liquidation value of the company which is distributed and the APR is observed absolutely. By contrast, in a reorganization procedure, more often than not, it is inevitable to deviate from the APR so that to achieve a settlement among the creditors and the debtors. The negotiations generate a kind of wealth redistribution in the sense that the debtors could keep their ownership position in the company in exchange to a revaluation of the unsecured debts at the expense of the secured ones. In other words, the secured creditors would not be paid off absolutely prior to the other unsecured creditors thereby leaving a room for maneuver to the company management to a restructuring and to a carrying on with the operation. This chapter summarizes the results of a primary research - carried out by Éva Pálinkó Deliné - which invesitagted that, although the Hungarian rules are seemingly in line with the international and regional standards and the EU regulations in reorganization matters, yet there, however, is no efficient capital allocation which would be expected by investors and which would be necessary to reinforce the trust in the market. The main argument of the chapter relying on this research is that Hungarian bankruptcy rules fail to promote efficient capital allocation because the stakeholders have no information or are not interested - as the costs may be too high - in those financial data or parameters, which are necessary for a deliberated settlement in a bankruptcy procedure. As a last resort, the deviation from the absolute priority rule (APR) may motivate the different classes of the creditors to enter an agreement on reorganization. Yet, the primary research analyzed in the underlying research shows that not even a deviation from the APR provides for a better environment for the settlement so that to save a value producing viable company. Generally, all companies with such a settlement in the research ended up, after some years, in a liquidation procedure or remained dormant in a non-active status.

1. Introduction

Absolute priority rule (APR) enables the secured creditors to receive full compensation (absolute) whereas others in the queue may receive nothing (priority),

[23] This chapter heavily relies on the findings of a case study carried out by Éva Pálinkó Deliné, at the Budapest Regional Capital Court, in Hungary between 2009-2017. The full research was published: Pálinkó, É., Pétervári, K. (2019). Creditors' Settlement or When Is It Advisable to Deviate from the Absolute Priority Rule. *Deturope*. 11(3): 264-282.

because the debtor's assets do not provide enough coverage. This rule is to yield more credit for debtors by lowering the secured creditors' risk. Critics of the APR emphasize that secured creditors are not motivated to negotiate the reorganization with non-secured creditors for a further operation of the company even if it were more efficient than final liquidation.

For avoiding the high transaction costs most of the legal orders in Europe render provisions against APR, the so called carve-out regulations. These regulations separate the debtors' assets and constraints the effectivity of the APR only partially.

The application of these rules become even more complex in case of crisis where bankruptcy is not necessarily the result of the inefficient activity of a company. In the crisis of the 1990s a more malleable system of reorganization was promoted everywhere. The lesson has been learned from several cases, like the General Motors, Chrysler cases: the assets of a company is the most valuable in its entirety, in its producing capacity, and any piecemeal sales of it would just generate more losses. Reorganization, especially early and possibly quick reorganization (or a pre-pack) is a crucial issue in the procedure. Yet, if the procedure is to be so quick it may not be transparent enough and so the debtors in possession, like the management or the owners, may enrich themselves at the expense of other stakeholders not equipped with the needed information. Out of this fear there are basically no pre-pack rules in Central and Eastern Europe (McCormack et al 2016). Swiftness is important though, because the loss of the good-will of a company in bankruptcy is extremely detrimental, which extends to further losses: the loss of customers, the loss of trained employees and loss of taxes for the local authorities.

This tendency to promote reorganization as opposed to liquidation was reinforced during the global crisis of 2008. In a financial crisis, due to the chain debts or debt-queues, many companies end up in insolvency despite of their long-term viability or otherwise value-producing activity in a longer period of time. These companies therefore need to be allowed to settle with their creditors and be able to restructure their debts.

A World Bank Study of 2010 analysis the effectiveness of the reorganization rules of the various countries during the crisis (Crismizi et al 2010). The number of the reorganization procedures soared all over the world in 2008. "For instance, in 2009, the number of corporate bankruptcies in Japan was 13,306, an increase of 4.9% from 2008 (Teikoku Databank, 2010i); the number of corporate bankruptcies in the U.K. was 94,135, an annual increase of 5.88% (Ministry of Justice, 2010ii); and the number of corporate bankruptcies in Germany was 32,687, which represents an 11% annual increase from 29,291 insolvencies in 2008, though the volume of debt more than doubled (Statistisches Bundesamt Deutschland, Jahrbuch, 2009iii). In the United States in 2009, 60,837 businesses declared bankruptcy, representing a 40% increase in filings from 2008 (American Bankruptcy

Institute, 2010 iv)." (in: Crismizi et al., 2010. 4) These numbers in the EU are not so high since the companies received 8,3% state aid in 2009, thus only 6% of the financially distressed companies filed for bankruptcy. The highest rate of bankruptcy 9,9% was that of Hungary (Correa et al 2010).

The reorganization rules not only have to provide lower costs for the debtors and so more certainty for the creditors to collect – even if later –, but also to make sure that viable and desired transactions would come into existence. The costs of inefficiency is not only that the parties loose – either both or any of them –, but that it has further consequences in the social loss, which would have added up from the possible benefit of those contracts which had never been entered into therefore never performed.

This chapter summarizes the results of a primary research conducted between 2009 and 2014 by Éva Pálinkó Deliné. The question was that, although the Hungarian rules are seemingly in line with the international standards in reorganization matters, why is there no such efficient capital allocation as it should be expected by the investors and would be necessary to reinforce the trust in the market. The main statement of this chapter is that the Hungarian bankruptcy rules fail because the stakeholders have no or biased information – for the costs may be too high – in those financial criteria, which are necessary for a deliberated settlement in a bankruptcy procedure.

2. Reorganization and settlement v. liquidation / the reason for an Absolute PRiority rule

2.1. Reorganization in the global crisis

The institution of reorganization is a child of the late 19th century economic crisis and its inefficient bankruptcy procedures. From this point of view, bankruptcy is a natural element in the life-cycles of capitalism. The creditors and the debtors in a bankruptcy procedure are supposed to cooperate efficiently thereby letting the economy grow.

In a crisis, however, this may not go easily, so special advisors to the World Bank in the East-Asian crisis of the 1990s, suggested the introduction of the "super Chapter 11" (Miller and Stiglitz 1999). This was supposed to be a cure as a necessary macroeconomic shock-therapy. The aim of the "super Chapter 11" was in fact not to liquidate the financially distressed but otherwise viable companies but to motivate the creditors and debtors to settle, since individual negotiations in a crisis is more costly and difficult especially because of the inevitable rise of the free riding problem. If some creditors write off enough debts then some others would not need so. Yet, by the force of the law the negotiations become cheaper and certain. This method however, comes at a price: contracts need to be renegotiated.

As a result, the "super Chapter 11" helped in the crisis management in East-Asia because liquidation was not automatic and many companies could survive. Yet, it was also true, that several unviable companies could carry on for too long with their businesses even after the crisis (Claessens et al 2005).

Notwithstanding, "super Chapter 11" was certainly tainted with moral hazard (Miller and Stiglitz 1999), since this crisis management necessarily protects those directors and owners who were first to be blamed for the coming about of the crisis itself (Demirguc et al 2009). Some argued, that albeit it is not fair, this might persuade the creditors to calculate this sort of risk. This then would raise the interest rates for all though (Klapper et al 2006). Others show, that one of the criteria of economic growth is to liquidate ailing companies. Certainly, when innovation increases in a sector, then the general survival rate decreases among the companies. The actual exit of the inefficient companies from the market pushes the remaining ones to be more efficient.

Despite of the fact that, seemingly, there is no consent among the academics whether or not the enhancement of reorganization is necessary, it is true that most EU Member States have more malleable rules on bankruptcy cases than used to have (McCormack et al 2016). These reforms are all to impede the liquidation of still productive companies and to let non-producing companies exit as soon as possible (Crismizi et al 2010). To reduce the costs of a bankruptcy procedure is good for the creditors, and a settlement between the creditors and the debtors may ameliorate the financial situation of the company. The experiences of the global financial crisis in 2008 are analogous with those of the East-Asian and Latin-American ones in the 1990s.

2.2. When is it rational for the debtors and the creditors to make a settlement

Financially distressed companies may choose between liquidation (exit) and bankruptcy (reorganization). Such a choice is effective when the costs and the expectations are freely deliberated. Such a decision, in a perfect market, is effective when the company ends up in reorganization because it is capable to create profit.

In practice, the decisions are often distorted by information asymmetry therefore there is a potential risk that value destructing companies operate further based on a credit restructuring settlement, or else a still value producing company is liquidated.

Rules however, may change behavior in a non-perfect market. Yet, the question, which party has less or more information, depends not only on the regulations. The interpretation of the various data requires more expertise. There has been a tendency that the shareholders and the management is more likely to choose reorganization even if liquidation were more efficient due to the complex problem of costs and principal-agent questions. Owners and/or the management may keep their position and push the costs on to the creditors. Since information is not equally available, owners may ameliorate their financial position at the expense of the creditors. Shareholders vote for projects which they otherwise would not support if creditors would not finance them (Stiglitz 1972). On the other hand the management is also interested in keeping its status so it advocates even risky investments in order to avoid bankruptcy. Therefore creditors in defense wish to push the costs of the management to the owners (fiduciary duty). In these cases if the creditors write off certain claims, the debtor may be able to stabilize the company and restructure the debt.).

To solve the information asymmetry problems some support the swift sale of the ailing company on the open market and the immediate compensation of the creditors according to the absolute priority rule (Eckbo and Thorburn 2009a). The residuum will be distributed to the owners, if any. The new owners then are the best fit to have a full informed decision on what to do with the company (this is like the Swedish mandatory auction bankruptcy procedure).

The whole debate on liquidation or reorganization has finally been erased by the global financial crisis of 2008. Although there are many more new ideas for the efficiency of the reorganizations, the basic notion as described is still fundamental.

2.3. When is it legally advisable to deviate from the APR

Bankruptcy laws are to enforce contracts from a strict legal point of view. Promises have to be fulfilled, if not, there are consequences. However, the idea of an efficient breach of contract is recognized ever since the promise was said to be no more than a prediction, that one must pay damages if broke his promise[24]. So it can be argued, that foreseeability and prediction is salient and the access to information is by far the most important issue.

Yet, information is not equally distributed among the interested parties. Secured creditors are always better informed than the non-secured (generally commercial) creditors, the employees or the other stakeholders. Beside, although owners, shareholders, investors or creditors of the company risk their wealth, they basically have no, or much less, information about the companies' future than the directors have, because they have chosen not to have (daily) access to it. Their

[24] This limit on the unanticipated transfers to the creditor could prevent industrial collapse in the borrowing country, but it raises the concerns of equity, specifically the fairness of changing the rules in mid-stream. To some degree, these claims may be outweighed by the greater imperative of maintaining production in the crisis. But "the rules" themselves are inherently ambiguous in the midst of a situation that neither party to the contract explicitly agreed upon or even envisioned.

agents are the directors who, however, tend to have inherently different, often rather short-term, interests; therefore directors owe special duty, the fiduciary duty, towards the company (i.e. agency problem). Hence the company laws and bankruptcy laws vest different rights into the owners (shareholders) to control the directors. The most important of those are the various obligations of the directors for disclosures, such as financial statements, balance sheets, convening the general meeting if the registered capital decreases, etc.

Early information, therefore is extremely precious. Already the threat of a compulsory disclosure could prevent certain bad investments, compelling the management to argue and deliberate. The directors' liability, the fiduciary duty (duty of care and duty of loyalty), also serve basically this purpose. Early information could preclude possible frauds, void contracts, like fraudulent conveyance, such as siphoning off the assets from the company, or other voidable contracts, such as illegally promoting certain creditors at the expense of others.

So the basic question of bankruptcy laws is who among the interested parties can get information, when and to what extent so that to make the necessary decisions. And then what measures could be used.

The interested parties in bankruptcy procedures are extremely diverse and in case the company is in the vicinity of bankruptcy, the stakeholders' roles often change. In the European legal regime, the directors cease to be liable only to the company. In some countries, among them Hungary, already the threat of bankruptcy causes the directors to be liable to the creditors rather, than to the company. So the law in paper provides for an early information to the creditors. After filing for bankruptcy, often they are even replaced or at least supervised by an appointee of the court. By contrast in US common law the debtor could remain in position (DIP = debtor in possession) and there is no automatic stay, which means that the directors can carry on with the business and the creditors are barred from rushing to collect. Creditors may, of course, sue afterwards but the assets of the company are not to be frozen in the USA. Generally, the opposite is true in Europe.

This is an important difference, if the creditors are not stopped from collecting after filing, then, instead of a possible reorganization of an otherwise viable company, the firm may end up in liquidation: the company is not protected from its creditors.

This is even more so when the APR applies. Secured creditors (senior creditors) with absolute priority contracts are first to be satisfied 100% (in Germany or Sweden) or less (in France) but still in first place (McCormack et al 2016). More often than not, bank loans are secured contracts, whereas commercial loans are not. Unsecured creditors (junior creditors) are at the rear of the queue, way after employees, tax authorities, landlords, etc. They therefore are not very likely to be able to collect. Hence they have an interest in reorganization rather than liquidation, but they have less bargaining power. The outcomes of the laws giving them voting power in a reorganization plan vary according to the diversity of the stakeholders.

Creditors are ranked, because transactions have prices. The contracting parties may decide how expensive their contracts should be. A secured contract is not at all cheap to draft. The parties (creditors definitely) think the risk is so high that it is worth investing more in drawing up such a contract. The use of standard terms can nevertheless reduce costs. Unsecured contracts are on the other hand cheap and quick contracts, parties feel they are not worth the trouble. The longer the time that elapses between the formation and the performance of the contract, the more likely it is for the parties to require certain securities.

If creditors are ranked, the classes – into which they are grouped for the purposes of bankruptcy procedures – gain significance. However, if there can be no negotiations about the APR among the creditors, then there is no motivation for the unsecured creditors to approve a reorganization plan if the company has not enough assets, so again the company faces liquidation instead of reorganization. Unsecured creditors suffer more of capital insufficiency and information asymmetry, hence a quick partial payback is often more crucial for their survival than a lengthy waiting time for a possible more. If the APR may be bargained over, meaning that the secured classes may waive their absolute right for priority satisfaction, then it is more likely that the various classes of creditors will be interested in a possible reorganization plan with a greater possible pay-back. Furthermore, if a creditor has to pay too high a registration charge for filing his unsecured claim, then he will not even show up, since there is no point in throwing his money after assets held under a regime that rigidly protects other creditors' interests with APR.

To achieve a settlement among the creditors the support of the majority based on the value of the claims is needed in only a few states in Central and Eastern Europe, e.g. in Slovakia, Bulgaria and in Hungary. In contrast, generally, a decision on such a settlement may be supported by both the majority of the number of the creditors and also the majority based on the value of the claims, like the Czech Republic, Poland and Romania. (McCormack et al 2016).

There are plenty of external costs in the business of a company, so owners are not the ultimate risk bearers as they used to be. The limited liability of shareholders/owners and the separate legal entity of the company makes businesses legally possible at the expense of others. If a financially distressed company files for bankruptcy, the rules allocating the risks are salient, since it is obviously possible that the (remaining) assets of the company will be distributed among its shareholders.

Thus distribution of the assets may be best prevented by the directors. They have the information on time. Therefore civil law sanctions apply in most of the countries in Central and Eastern Europe, if directors fail to file for bankruptcy in time and so they cause damages. These are: Czech Republic, Slovenia and Estonia. Beside civil liability however many countries introduced criminal sanctions too, like Croatia, Bulgaria, Latvia, Poland and Romania. Interestingly enough, only in Hungary and Slovakia in Central Europe, where there are no such rules (McCormack et al 2016). Even more interestingly, however, in case creditors sustained losses as a result of mismanagement of the assets in the jeopardy of the bankruptcy, directors have to compensate the creditors.

In any event, the biggest problem in the continent is the liability of the directors and their not being motivated to disclose information early, because in case of bankruptcy they lose control and are removed from their positions. On the other hand, the directors of the SMEs are the owners themselves, so information is definitely at hand. In these cases these are the creditors – secured or unsecured – who need information desperately in time.

2.4. When is it financially advisable to deviate from the APR?

A special cooperation of the creditors is needed if the coverage (the collateral security) is not enough for all the claims of an otherwise viable debtor. Such settlements mostly require the majority, or even the qualified majority of the creditors or of the creditors representing the majority or qualified majority of the amount of all claims. Therefore, the question is, whether the secured creditors could be motivated to settle not only with the debtor but also with other unsecured creditors, by writing off certain amount of their claims so that to inspire the unsecured creditors too to vote for the settlement. This willingness of the secured creditors to write off some of their claims can be motivated either individually by a renegotiation of the secured contract between the debtor and the creditor or generally by the power of the law. This latter could regulate that in case of a bankruptcy the coverage should not be absolute and prior, rendering APR to be unobserved ipso iure (the carve-out).

The assets of an ailing company are to be divided differently among the various classes of creditors if it is decided in a reorganization or in a liquidation procedure. During liquidation it is the liquidation value of the company which is distributed and the APR is observed absolutely. By contrast, in a reorganization procedure, more often than not, it is inevitable to deviate from the APR so that to achieve a settlement among the creditors and the debtors. The negotiations generate a kind of wealth redistribution in the sense that the debtors could keep their ownership position in the company in exchange to a revaluation of the unsecured debts at the expense of the secured ones. In other words, the secured creditors would not be paid off absolutely prior to the other unsecured creditors thereby leaving a room for maneuver to the company management to a restructuring and to a carrying on with the operation.

The objective of a reorganization procedure is to focus on the further operation of the company. This means that the management still owes a fiduciary duty towards the company. By contrast, in a liquidation procedure the interest of the creditors comes forward and takes over the fiduciary duty of the management towards the company.

Depending on the bargaining positions of the creditors – and based on equal access to information for all participants –, if liquidation were more advantageous to the owners and the unsecured creditors than the reorganization, then the secured creditors might be more motivated to negotiate for a settlement in case of a viable company. The unsecured creditors, like suppliers, are often more interested in a quick partial pay off than a lengthy waiting period of hoping for more. Therefore the deviation from the APR is a fundamental issue in reorganizations.

This however requires the renegotiations of the existing contracts. The question is the ratio between the positive effect of the possible settlement together with the further value producing operation of the company and the costs of the breaching of the APR, i.e. the costs to get creditors with priority be involved in writing off credits (in the hope of a higher return).

Obviously, the APR is a very important instrument for providing credit, therefore its breach or a renegotiation in the bankruptcy procedure will have even ex ante impact on the financing costs of the company.

Truly a deviation from the APR may result in a positively effective reallocation of company assets so that the shareholders keep their investment in the restructured company, the creditors undertake the refinancing and the strategic suppliers (generally the non-secured creditors) support the company as a going concern, etc. None of these potential benefits should veil the fact that any deviation from the APR comes at a price which is to be calculated at the time of deciding on the creditors' settlement.

Therefore a settlement for reorganization – and thereby a deviation from the APR – is to be supported unless and until the degree of the deviation would result in a pricing change of the value producing companies in the financial markets (at the expense of the minority shareholders in the ailing companies).

3. The effect of the Hungarian bankruptcy amendments based on the empirical research of Éva Pálinkó Deliné

These were also the salient questions of the primary research carried out after the global crisis in Hungary by Éva Pálinkó Deliné. The basic issue was that there is no clear shift in the reorganization data after the new rules on reorganization were introduced in 2009. Although these rules are seemingly in line with the international standards in reorganization matters (law in paper), still there is no such efficient capital allocation as should have been expected by the investors and would have been necessary to reinforce the trust in the market (law in action).

The Act No. LI of 2009 in Hungary, amended the then existing bankruptcy rules and promoted reorganization procedures as opposed to liquidation. But the intent to reinvigorate the institution of bankruptcy in general met only accidentally with the aim of the globally enhanced preferences. This provision was a result of a more than a decade long debate during the transition from the socialist command market to a free market. The first step, back then, was to introduce a uniquely strict automatic bankruptcy law as a response to the reluctance of the companies to file for bankruptcy or liquidation (Act No XLIX of 1991). The rules therein on promoting automatic stay which could help creditors' settlement (collateral settlement) were withdrawn in 1993, since then companies in financial distress systemically faced liquidation. This practice was to be changed to promote reorganization in 2009 again (Act No. LI of 2009). The priority of the reorganization procedure over liquidation was declared anew, an automatic stay rule (immediate moratorium) was reintroduced.

According to the findings, the goals of the new laws on the reorganization plan did not work. If the aim was to elaborate a plan how to re-establish the liquidity of a company for continued short-term operation with due regard to the market environment and the company's potentials, then it was plainly not working. This included the lack of plans for the collecting of receivables and the sale of assets without jeopardizing the short-term financing of operations to be continued. Neither were the portfolio services adjusted to the (new future) market expectations and the long-term financing of the company needs. Nor were there plans to ensure the resources for the restructuring company or any optimization of the capital leverage. There were simply no reorganization plan to indicate how to reach a profitable company structure efficiently and whether to sell the assets of the company in toto or piece by piece.

Those findings show conspicuously that the high repayment expectations in the creditors' settlements are not fulfilled. The majority of the companies with settlement become either non-operating or liquidated. This is also clear, that the new bankruptcy regulations of the global crisis grant neither an efficient reallocation in the reorganization procedure nor a better rate of claims repayment by the deviation from the APR. These results are mirrored in the decreasing numbers of the filing for bankruptcies with the bankruptcy courts in a period between 2008 and 2017.

4. Efficiency of the hungarian bankruptcy rules in the eu context

The rational beyond the shift in the regulation in Hungary, was that in the case of a financially distressed company a flexible reorganization procedure should ameliorate, complement – replace or forestall, if needed – the bankruptcy procedures resulting in liquidation. Yet, the primary research cited in this chapter shows that not even the breach of the APR provides for a better environment for the settlement. Generally all companies with such a settlement in the research ended up, after a few years, in a liquidation procedure or remained dormant in a non-active status. Thus, in Hungary, systemically, reorganizations do not set up value producing viable companies.

Clearly, these problems do not root in the regulations: bankruptcy laws do comply with the EU regulations and the international standards. The reasons for this system failure – according to the primary research, are rather (i) the structure of the financial/credit market, (ii) the overwhelming majority of the SMEs as opposed to companies listed in the stock market and (iii) the nature of the credit for the SMEs.

The Hungarian financial market is bank-based market. Market participants seldom collect money from the public through the stock market. In fact, the setting up of a public company directly in the stock market is illegal (Civil Code 3:249. §).

Graph 1.

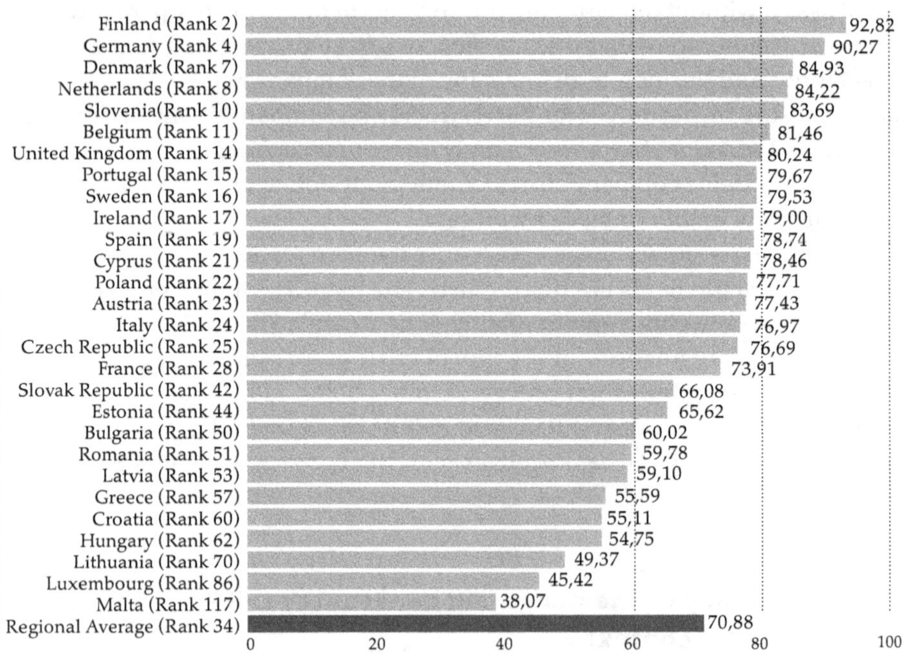

Source: Doing Business database 2017.

The research of Éva Pálinkó Deliné has proved that almost half of the companies in the bankruptcy procedure lacked secured credits, which means that these companies had no bank loans at all. These debtors faced commercial creditors, consumers, taxpayers or simply employees. These commercial creditors, often in financial distress themselves too, cannot make settlements, especially, because for them often there is no information in hand whatsoever. The bank-based financial markets are not too transparent, but a market full with SMEs, is even more blur. Because of the big numbers of the SMEs in the market and often because of the lack of capacity to understand financial risks from the commercial creditors' or the employees' part, the rational basis of a creditors' settlement is far from realistic.

Therefore the amended Hungarian bankruptcy laws in compliance with the EU regulation could not guarantee a better ranking for the country. As is seen in Graph 1, the efficiency of the bankruptcy rules in Hungary provides only the 25th place among the 28 Member States, far below the EU average. Clearly, the law in paper is not what the law in action is.

5. Conclusion

This promotion of conditional reorganization as opposed to liquidation in the past few decades was designed to achieve a competitive position in the global markets. Unsurprisingly, it is the US Chapter 11 reorganization rule which serve as good business standard in most European countries and the Member States of the EU as well.

Even if it is the same rational, it functions differently in a bank-based, creditor-friendly financial market dominated mostly by SMEs not being eligible for bank-loans. The rules in Hungary therefore differ from those in paper to those in action. In the latter one even the bankruptcy laws ensure traditionally that a troubled company be liquidated and the creditors be paid up as soon as possible. Hence the results are not yet to be seen as wished for.

REFERENCES

1. Barnett, K. (2012): *Accounting for Profit for Breach of Contract*. Theory and Practice. Hart Publishing. 256.
2. Blazy, R., Petey, J., Weill, L. (2018): Serving the creditors after insolvency filings: from value creation to value distribution. *Eur J Law Econ* 45 pp.331–375 https://doi.org/10.1007/s10657-017-9560-9
3. Boon, G. (2018): Harmonising EU Insolvency Law: The Emerging Role of Stake-holders. Int'l Insolv. Rev Vol 27:150-177 Wiley online

4. Cirmizi, E., Klapper, L. and Uttamachandi, M. (2010): The Challenges of Bankruptcy Reform. *The World Bank*, October WPS5448 http://dx.doi.org/10.1596/1813-9450-5448)
5. Claessens, S., Laeven, L. (2005): Financial Dependence, Banking Sector Competition, and Economic Growth. *Journal of the European Economic Association*, Vol.3. No. 1. pp.179-207 http://dx.doi.org/10.1162/1542476053295322
6. Correa, P., Iootty, M., (2010): The Impact of the Global Economic Crisis on the Corporate Sector in Europe and Central Asia: Evidence from a Firm-Level Survey. *Enterprise Surveys Enterprise Note Series. EU 10 Regular Economic Report, the World Bank Group.* http://documents.worldbank.org/curated/en/742641468022737863/The-impact-of-the-global-economic-crisis-on-the-corporate-sector-in-Europe-and-Central-Asia-evidence-from-a-firm-level-survey
7. Csőke, A. (ed.) (2009): *A csődtörvény magyarázata.* (Commentary on the Act of Bankruptcy) Complex Kiadó.
8. Deliné Pálinkó, É., Pétervári, K. (2019). Creditors' Settlement or When Is It Advisable to Deviate from the Absolute Priority Rule. *Deturope*. 11(3): 264-282
9. Demirgüç-Kunt, Asli, Laeven, L, and Levine, R. (2004): Regulations, Market Structure, Institutions, and the Cost of Financial Intermediation. *Journal of Money, Credit and Banking*, 36, 593–622. https://www.jstor.org/stable/pdf/3838956.pdf?refreqid=excelsior%3A83c1e2af1342b4b58fc49e279798ec4a
10. Eberhart, A., Weiss, L. (1998): The Importance of Deviations from the Absolute Priority Rule in Chapter 11 Bankruptcy Proceedings, *Financial Management* 27(4) February 1998 DOI: 10.2307/3666416
11. Eckbo, E. and Thorburn, K. (2002): Control Benefits and CEO Discipline in Automatic Bankruptcy Auctions. *CEPR Discussion Paper* No. 3481. https://ssrn.com/abstract=330562
12. Eckbo, E. and Thorburn K., (2009a): Economic Effects of Auction Bankruptcy. *Tuck School of Business Working Paper* No. 2009-63 http://ssrn.com/abstract=1387347
13. Eckbo, E. and Thorburn, K., (2009b): Creditor financing and overbidding in bankruptcy auctions: Theory and tests. *Journal of Corporate Finance* 15 pp.10–29.
14. Gine, X., Love, I. (2010): Do Reorganization Costs Matter for Efficiency? Evidence from a Bankruptcy Reform in Colombia. *The Journal of Law and Economics*, Vol. 53, No. 4. pp. 833-864. http://dx.doi.org/10.1086/605848
15. Klapper, L., Laevena, L., Rajan, R. (2006): Entry Regulation as a Barrier to Entrepreneurship. *Journal of Financial Economics*, 82. pp.591–629. http://dx.doi.org/10.1016/j.jfineco.2005.09.006
16. Longhofer, S. and Carlstrom, C. (1995): Absolute Priority Rule Violations in Bankruptcy. *Economic Review*. FRB Cleveland. http://clevelandfed.org/research/review/
17. McCormack, G., Brown, S., Keay, A., Dahlgreen, J., (2016) *Study on a new approach to business failure and insolvency Comparative legal analysis of the Member States' relevant provisions and practices.* Tender No. JUST/2014/JCOO/PR/CIVI/0075 ISBN 978-92-79-58019-2 doi:10.2838/87512 DS-02-16-331-EN-N. 464.
18. McCormack, G. (2017): Business restructuring law in Europe: making a fresh start. *Journal of Corporate Law Studies*. Volume 17, 2017 – Issue 1
19. Miller, M. and Stiglitz, J. (1999) Bankruptcy protection against macroeconomic shocks: the case for a 'super Chapter 11'. *World Bank revised draft*, December, 1999.

20. Roe, M., Tung, F. (2013): Breaking Bankruptcy Priority: How Rent-Seeking Upends the Creditors' Bargain' 99 *Virginia Law Review* 1235.

21. Senbet, L., Wang, T. (2012): Corporate financial distress and bankruptcy: A survey. *Foundations and Trends® in Finance* http://dx.doi.org/10.1561/0500000009

22. Stiglitz, J. (1972): Some respects of the Pure Theory of Corporate Finance Bankrupticies. *Management Science*. Autumn, 3. 458-482.

23. Thorburn, K. (2000): Bankruptcy auctions: Costs, debt recovery and firm survival, *Journal of Financial Economics* 58, 337-368., http://dx.doi.org/10.1016/s0304-405x(00)00075-1

CHAPTER 3.

RISKS OF LEGAL ELITES IN LEGISLATIVE DRAFTING

The fifth chapter addresses the question of legislation. Even though legal experts do not create legislation, it is appropriate to question the role that different legal professionals—attorneys (advocate lawyers), judges, prosecutors, law professors, law clerks in the government administration, etc.—play in drafting law. Assuming that creating the law requires real power, one should be able to discern which group of professionals exerts the most influence on this process. Depending on the cultural values of a community, the expectation that people play by the rules is more or less strong, with the effect that an individual who has intentionally violated the rules may or may not feel compelled to justify or apologize for their behavior. It is also well established that playing by the rules is best accomplished if one has the power to create and modify these rules, perhaps even retroactively. Laws and regulations are no different from this, with one exception: their binding nature—which, of course, implies enforcement—means that creating laws requires genuine power. it is more likely than not that academics are the best equipped legal professional group, because they have the opportunity to disguise their own group interests by pretending their sociological identity as representatives of objectivity, using scientific methodology, and legal rationality.

1. Introduction

Even though legal experts do not create legislation, it is appropriate to question the role that different legal professionals—attorneys (advocate lawyers), judges, prosecutors, law professors, law clerks in the government administration, etc.—play in drafting law[25]. Assuming that creating the law requires real power, one should be able to discern which group of professionals exerts the most influence on this process.

Depending on the cultural values of a community, the expectation that people play by the rules is more or less strong, with the effect that an individual who has intentionally violated the rules may or may not feel compelled to justify or apologize for their behavior. It is also well established that playing by the rules is best accomplished if one has the power to create and modify these rules, perhaps even retroactively. Laws and regulations are no different from this, with one exception: their binding nature—which, of course, implies enforcement—means that creating laws requires genuine power.

---

25 Cserne and Gajduschek, *"Jogalkotási javaslatok,"* 80–83.

The traditional view in Hungary is that Hungarian law, like German law, is a so-called *Professorenrecht*—that is, the laws of both states are drafted by academics[26]. Thus, professors of various universities and research institutes are usually recognized as the most influential legal elite within the broad definition of the legal profession. However, I argue that the struggle for leverage in the process has become more subtle and complex over time. Clearly, the power of drafting laws among different groups of legal professionals depends not only on legal networks or on the structure of the legal systems, but also on the historical, cultural, economic, and sociological environment in which they operate. These circumstances have dramatically changed since the Second World War both in (post-)socialist regimes and in constitutional democracies, especially due to the internationalization of laws in an increasingly globalized world[27]. In order to account for this transformation and reorientation of the legal systems, my analysis uses the broad expression of "creating the law," which is not a terminus technicus, per se[28]. Further, because of the complicated problem of who wields agenda-setting power in politics, the various legal systems and the legal branches within these systems react differently[29]. Undoubtedly, one distinguishes the common law tradition and the continental European approach to law creation. Even though the concept of a positivist written law, which entailed the participation of a professorial elite in the legislative process, became widespread in the past several decades, the necessary interpretation of these rules still provides certain leverage to other professional groups, especially judges. Further, the theoretical problem of how much creativity is implied in the application of law is not new.

Having said that, it is more likely than not that academics are the best equipped legal professional group, because they have the opportunity to disguise their own group interests by citing their sociological identity as representatives of objectivity, scientific methodology, and legal rationality[30]. Consequently, this analyzes of the legal elite in the legislative process in two parts. Part one focuses on the notion of *Professorenrecht* in the sphere of private/civil law, and specifically in the context of the legislative process that produced the new Hungarian Civil Code of 2013. The lengthy drafting process during this codification process is a good case study that shows the internal rivalries among the various legal profes-

---

[26] See Sárközy, *"A jog szerepe." Professorenrecht* has various meanings. Currently it is often used in a pejorative sense, referring to a "dogmatic style" that is hard to understand and "full of concepts and abstractions." In other words, it means that content is not accessible for nonspecialists. For example, see Hesselink, *The New European Private Law*, 95, 154. It may also be used as a possible tool for harmonization in EU private law. See Schepel, *"Professorenrecht?"* But *Professorenrecht* may have another abstract meaning too, namely that certain interpretations, perhaps new legal institutions may be codified in writing later, similar to the influence that law practice has on codification. See Menyhárd, *"A polgári jog tudománya,"* 226–45.

[27] Ip, *"Globalization."*

[28] This is important especially if one believes that the law cannot be made, but only modified.

[29] See, for example, Menyhárd, *"A polgári jog tudománya,"* 247–50.

[30] Sajó, *Kritikai értekezés*, 190.

sional groups such as bureaucrats, traditional legal professionals (judges and practicing lawyers), and academics. It also clarifies the specific Hungarian legislative process in the post–Second World War period, but reflects on earlier times thereby providing a necessary point of comparison. Part two tells the story of the birth of Hungary's 2012 Basic Law. In this case the participation of law professors in the drafting procedure was almost negligible. As such, it became representative of a new, definitively non-traditional way of creating law.

2. Private law

2.1. The notion of *Professorenrecht*

Historically, the particular feudal political and legal system of the German-Roman Empire eventually required a path to the harmonization of local case law with universal legal standards or principles. This task was then completed by professors in various universities where different and often competing legal theories had been elaborated on with great zeal (e.g., the exegists, the pandektists, the legal historians, etc.). In Hungary, this kind of standardization requirement took place much later and under very different political circumstances. Historically, so-called judges always represented customs, local customary laws, or particularized privileges. Their professional education began as late as the second half of the seventeenth century, when some form of legal studies were introduced in Hungarian higher education[31].

At that time, proper legal professionals (mostly non-Catholics) still studied abroad, and they became attorneys and professors having been barred access to the political administration and justice system[32]. These professionals represented modern legal thinking, especially the necessity of a written legal code. Oddly enough, this intent also mirrored the political agenda of the Habsburg emperors. Thus the struggle between the modernization or integration of the country into a broader economic area (a trading zone) on the one hand, and that of the stabilization of Hungarian leadership in the region and by extension the imposition of old customs on the other, created a delicate situation. This discrepancy of goals generated fairly clear dividing lines between legal professionals on the basis of their social origins[33]. Moreover, this environment was difficult to manage because of another conflict between the rigidly Catholic Habsburgs and the traditionally Protestant and/or re-Catholicized Hungarian nobility, whose desire for autonomy drove it to use anything one could as a bargaining chip in negotiations at court.

---

31 Mezey, "*A jogászképzés változásai*," 40; Szuromi, "*A középkori egyetemek létrejöttének*"; and Mezey, "*Jogalkotás*," 1–2.

32 Horváth, "*Tudós elmék*," 21–26; and Hamza, "*Vécsey Tamás*," 12–21.

33 Asztalos, "*A magyar burzsoá*."

The role of professors as the creators of law was obviously not an ancient custom in Hungary, but rather originated as a consequence of the Hungarian resistance to the Habsburg modernization. This German orientation was due to the fact that various (often subtle) forms of opposition or resistance to Habsburg influence could be expressed through the law, especially after 1867. These persistent opposites, however obscured, still exist—i.e., modernization versus customs; non-institutionalized freelancers versus political administration; the enlightened administration versus institutionalized academics. Thus, the roles of legal actors were interchangeable depending on the political, historical, and economic environment.

Nevertheless, the rare exceptions to the general rule were periods of major political rupture when the enlightened administration historically played the main role in making law: the foundation of the Dual Monarchy, Austria-Hungary, in 1867; and Hungary's accession to the European Union. Broadly speaking, in these kinds of struggles, judges historically may be characterized as agents of the administration, but definitely acted as the protectors of the status quo, whereas attorneys served as representatives of academic circles, which were open to modernization.

2.2. The biased development of private law in the era of feudalism (and beyond)

As discussed above, legal sources in Hungary were rooted in rules and systems of donation, customs, and written customary laws and privileges until as late as the mid-nineteenth century. These customs and written customary laws, such as the Golden Bull of 1222 or the Tripartitum of 1514, guaranteed the lengthy survival of the Hungarian-style (or Central European) feudal regime[34]. They extended the rights of the grand seigneurs (peerage; *főnemesség*) to all those with noble titles, thereby deflecting the classical feudal hierarchical contractual relationship among the king, peers, and servants, and creating a broad sociological strata of largely impoverished nobles (középnemesség), who lacked wealth but wielded political power. This proved handy for the Habsburg emperors (kings of Hungary after 1526) in their struggle for more leverage against the peerage and serfs (*jobbágy*), respectively. In exchange the nobility had no other interest but to maintain this feudal system as the status quo for as long as possible.

Due to global economic developments in the eighteenth and nineteenth centuries, written economic law invaded some parts of the established customary legal system in the entire Europe, including Hungary. These laws, mostly initiated

[34] The Golden Bull was meant for constitutional terms mostly (the rights of the nobilities against the king, e.g. the right of resistance), and the *Tripartitum* for private matters mostly (inheritance, contracts, system of donations, entail, etc.). See Szűcs, *Nemzet és történelem*.

by the Habsburgs, mainly reflected the needs of the emerging early capitalist market, such as new acts on the trading partnerships (*közkereseti társaság*), the bill of exchange (*váltó*), liquidation (*csőd*), etc[35]. The transformation of commercial law, however, left the private sphere of the noble classes intact until the revolution of 1848. Moreover, certain dimensions, mostly concerning property and related issues, such as the entail (*hitbizomány*), the donation system (*adományrendszer*), and noble classes' inheritance and family law, remained in force during the Horthy regime and even as late as 1949, mostly as customs applied by county courts (*táblabíróság*)[36].

Therefore, it is clear that the influence of written law had not touched the field of private law strictu sensu, but only commercial law. Commercial law was traditionally outside of the scope of the Tripartitum, since the noble classes had never been interested in trade. The nobles' judges and other legal clerks in the county administration could fortify their own power through the customs and privileges applied by the courts. This is the reason why the codification process of the Hungarian Civil Code took more than one hundred years after the 1848 revolution.

Written laws could only regulate credit, loans, and liens, for example, if they left the basic characteristics of the land system (entail, donation, inheritance) intact[37]. Notwithstanding, it should be noted that after the revolution of 1848, during the neo-absolutistic era, the land registry (*telekkönyv*) system was incorporated into the Hungarian legal system according to the Austrian Civil Code[38].

Despite the legal nullification of the bonded servant system (serfdom) in 1848, the family law and the contracts of the noble classes remain essentially the same governed by the customary laws of the Tripartitum. The application of the written laws of valorization related to property transactions (sales, inheritance, mortgages, etc.) during the economic crisis after the First World War and the laws created during the great depression in Hungary still had to wrestle with customary laws as applied by county courts with regard to older precedents[39].

---

35 See Act No. 1840: XVIII. tc. a közkereseti társaságról [on partnership]; Act No. 1840: XV.tc. a váltóról [on bills of exchange]; and Act No. 1840: XXII. tc. a csődületről [on insolvency].

36 See Act No. 1949. No. VII. tv. a hitbizományok megszüntetéséről [on the abolition of entail].

37 Once a land belonged to a noble, it could not be bought or inherited by a non-noble. Towns, especially agricultural towns (*mezőváros*), could not own "noble" lands until the 1840s. See Act No. 1844:IV.tc.

38 See Asztalos, *"A magyar burzsoá,"* 58.

39 See, for example, Bilét and Menyhért, *"A redintegrációról,"* 37–38.

2.3. When can we start talking about *Professorenrecht*?

Undoubtedly, one should only discuss Professorenrecht if there are "professors" worth mentioning. The academic sphere was not really a decisive part of the legal development of the Hungarian private law until the nineteenth century.

Illés Georch wrote the first legal book on private law in Hungarian in 1804, during a time when most scholars still communicated in Latin[40]. Notwithstanding the language, the legal literature of that time was simply a presentation of the country's customs and laws with added commentary[41]. Universities were not the most important places for legal education and training. Rather, students obtained their knowledge through practice or internships (patvaria) at local law firms or in the local administration. Since most judges and the law clerks came from the noble classes, their instruction depended on traditional, customary (written) law.

There was a strong discrepancy in the legal thinking between these lawyers and those who represented the interests of the towns and traders later on in the nineteenth century. The latter group attended proper legal courses at foreign universities and practiced mostly as attorneys or journalists. Their controversies might be described with an analogical reference to the debate between Thibaut and Savigny, though with a decisive distinction[42]. Under the influence of the French revolutionary ideas of 1789 and their embodiment in the Civil Code, both Thibaut and Savigny recognized the need for legal reform in the divided German states. However, whereas Thibaut advocated for a new codification, Savigny insisted on incremental reforms to the evolutionary, historical, organic development of German law. The controversy caused by these lawyers' rival notions never really exploded in Hungary where there was no actual debate until 1861.[43] Even then, there was no consensus on the form that necessary reforms should take[44].

After the defeat of the revolution of 1848, it is intriguing to observe how lawyers used the legal system to struggle for independence from the Habsburg Empire. This was the exact period when German law (especially Prussian), as opposed to the Austrian example, emerged as a major reference point for Hungarian lawmakers. After having repealed the 1848–1849 revolutionary legislation, the emperor ordered the Austrian Civil Code to be implemented in Hungarian territories, which outraged the majority of practicing lawyers who opted for the old (unreformed) customary law.

---

40 Georch, *Honnyi törvény I–II.*

41 See Asztalos, "*A magyar burzsoá,*" 29.

42 See the debate in Peschka, "*Thibaut és Savigny vitája.*"

43 See Asztalos, "A magyar burzsoá," 30. The two radical positions in this debate are exemplified by Ignác Frank (1788–1850), who taught at the Pázmány Péter University, and László Szalay (1813–1864), who was a journalist and a delegate of the Centrum Party at the Frankfurt General Meeting.

44 Ráth, *Az Országbírói Értekezlet.*

2.4. The rivalry among legal elites in the legislative process for private law after 1848

Having realized that the traditional customary laws had been restored, which hindered the economic integration of the country and halted its development, the emperor commanded the chief judge to summon a General Meeting (*Országbírói Értekezlet*) of upper judges (*táblabíró*), peers, and lawyers. The objective was to reconcile Hungarian customs with the Austrian Civil Code. In 1861, the General Meeting was organized by the chief judge (judex curiae regiae). According to the documents there were sixteen lawyers, fourteen members of the clergy and the nobility, five upper judges, and five representatives of the commoners, chambers, and traders. These numbers demonstrate that while peers and judges were overrepresented, academics were nowhere to be found among those who attended the meeting[45]. The primary representatives belonged to the established estates (the clergy and the noble classes), while only a few commoners were present. However, this meeting marked a turning point, namely the beginning of Hungary's coerced modernization process.

The outcome of this meeting was a genuine compromise. Instead of drafting new laws, the compromise entailed the very limited acceptance of the Austrian Civil Code (basically only the land registry and the mining provisions) and very limited reforms to written customary laws (especially in the field of commercial law, e.g., the bill of exchange). The peerage consented to the land registry system, which provided them with greater and safer access to credit, and the nobility were able to exempt their territories from commerce. The real nature of this compromise might well be illustrated by the contradictory results in family law.

While serfdom (*jobbágyság*) legally ceased to exist after 1848 and (formal) equality before the law was recognized, due to the reinforcement of customary law, family law, and especially inheritance laws, the distinction among different noble classes and serfs was maintained[46]. Interestingly enough, more radical young lawyers who later became important legal clerks in the administration and even influential politicians represented the commoners' lawyers[47]. All the rules agreed upon at the General Meeting were collected under the title of "Temporary Applicable Rules" (*Ideiglenes Törvénykezési Szabályok*) and remained in effect for the next century, until 1959.

After having passed the law on the conciliation of Austria and Hungary in 1867,[48] the struggle for an independent legal system continued as before and often at the expense of national economic interests. This struggle was legitimized by traditional judges (local and county), since there were no new written laws,

[45] Ibid.

[46] See paternal or maternal inheritance.

[47] For example Boldizsár Horváth, who later served as Minister of Justice, and Ferenc Deák, who was the mastermind and the chief negotiator of the Austro-Hungarian Compromise of 1867.

[48] See Act No. 1867:XII.tc.

and—when such laws existed—they were simply considered to be anomalies in the system of case law, ready to be applied (possibly with deference) to customary laws. Loopholes were supposed to be filled in with scholarly legal works authored by the professoriate. "Multipositioning" was very common among different legal elites in developed cities, especially Budapest[49]. Attorneys or judges often received honorary titles from the university (*címzetes magántanár*), and they often published scholarly studies. This situation remained fundamentally intact until the Second World War. Therefore, one might assert that Hungary's *Professorenrecht* did not share the same attributes as its German counterpart. There was no *Professorenrecht strictu sensu*, because academics did not occupy similar positions as those in Germany at the time. The selection of law professors was not an autonomous right of the faculty; they had to be approved by the Ministry of Justice, and negotiations between the two camps were seldom smooth50. The staff of universities was often recruited from among the traditional higher judges (*táblabíró*) who gave preference to customary law[51]. It should also be noted that during the Austro-Hungarian Monarchy, the enlightened governments seem to have been in constant conflict with academic appointees. The state administration (Ministry of Justice) and (freelance) urban lawyers were specifically advocated for the complex codification and reform of the private law[52]. Clashes concerning nominations in the law faculties and colleges often developed between the faculty and the administration.

These generally resulted in a compromise or in the abrupt creation of new departments[53]. This antagonism, which was characteristic of professional legal elites in Hungary, extended well into the twentieth century.

2.5. The Civil Code that was never codified (1867-1945)

The codification of Hungary's complex civil code took more than thirty years to draft, and although several versions reached the plenary sessions of Parliament, they were never passed. This mirrors the ambiguous public approach to the modernization agenda in the country. Around the end of the nineteenth century,

49 Károly Csemegi may serve as a good example. He was basically everything during his career (lawyer, law clerk, high official administrator, and judge), but when he was asked to draft the Penal Code, he was given a high office in the Ministry of Justice.

50 The Pázmány Péter Faculty of Law was a state owned, yet autonomous institution (on paper). Mezey, "*Wlassics Gyula.*"

51 See, for example, Gusztáv Wenzel (1812–1891), a follower of Ignác Frank. Wenzel was a professor.

52 For example, István Telesky (1836–1899), a State Secretary at the Ministry of Justice, or Rezső Dell'Adami (1850–1888), a lawyer and honorary professor. His habilitation was suspended by Wenzel who claimed his research, which demonstrated customary laws were influenced by different legal systems such as Roman and German law, was antinational.

53 See the history of the criminal law department and the case of Wlassics Gyula, in Mezey, "*Wlassics Gyula.*"

traditional (still feudal) ruling nobilities lost ground against commoners representing the industrial and commercial elite of Hungary, and this group became increasingly stubborn in its resistance to the legal revision of its customs. Business and commerce were once again regarded as "non-Hungarian," and consequently, new laws regarding merchant activity were to remain separate from the traditional legal system.

Documents show that there were six academics, two lawyers, one prosecutor, two judges, and six bureaucrats and clerks working on the drafting[54]. This demonstrates that the influence of two groups in this stage of the legal codification process, bureaucrats and academics, remained balanced. It is telling that despite the fact that the Ministry of Justice had often been the real engine of legal reform, revisions to private law were rarely adopted because of the resistance of traditionalist county law clerks who were overrepresented in Parliament.

Oddly enough, the draft was in operation as a recommendation or a set of guidelines for courts to follow. Similar to the legal basis of the Tripartitum, the Private Law Draft (MTK javaslat) also acted like written customary law, was cited by judges, and affected case law in Hungary. On a practical level, this meant that the former dual (coexistent) regime of private law continued to prevail. The written, ad-hoc commercial law statutes performed the role of subsidiary laws for cases in which customary laws could provide no resolution to the problems in question (e.g., the obligations, contracts, liability, etc.). Thus, fundamental laws of liberal capitalism related to the protection of private property, freedom of contract, and equality before the law, could only be partially instrumentalized. The crisis of capitalism and the problems of "monopolistic capitalism" (imperialism) later on often served as a pretext for the revival of old customary law, including anti-competition laws, usury, debtors' protection, and inequality before the law.

2.6. The rivalry of legal elites after the Second World War

As is well known, the overall conditions of political and professional decision-making changed radically within the Soviet system after 1945. Paradoxically enough, this led to the finalization of the draft and passage of the new and very first Hungarian Civil Code. The final version applied certain tenets of the former Private Law Draft (MTK javaslat) along with former case law, although it placed both in an undoubtedly socialist context[55]. But a written, codified Civil Code, as in Act No. IV of 1959, was not at all self-evident, even in the positivist legal environment of normative socialism. The code entered into effect on January 1, 1960.

---

[54] Source: ELTE, Department of Hungarian Legal History.

[55] See the opinion of Imre Szabó on the Civil Code in a debate at the Institute for Legal Studies, in "*A Ptk. Tervezetének vitája*."

Crucial changes in the legal system had already been made by then, and the code had to transform customary law into written private law within a new legal environment.

The legislative committees had eight academic members and thirteen bureaucrats and clerks. The academics were totally outnumbered by bureaucrats in the administration and by party experts[56]. It should be noted that the former possibility of "multipositioning" across different groups of legal elites ceased to exist, and lawyers—especially attorneys—became a suspicious cluster (category/box X: outsiders in the tripartite party-state of workers, peasants, and "progressive intellectuals"). Academics, however, were very welcome in the drafting and interpreting of law, for want of legitimacy within the regime.

After the Second World War, the legal system underwent obvious changes. The role of judges became much less important since they were no longer needed to interpret law or customs. By the same token, the role of the academics grew because written law required arguments. The new drafting process needed both analysis and interpretation of the current situation in Hungary, and a vision of the desired future. Academics were the best suited and equipped for this job. Thus, paradoxically, Professorenrecht may have become more a feature of the legal system in Hungary after the Second World War than before. From this period on, academics involved in law creation included members of newly founded research institutions. Researchers had no effect on the training of further generations of legal scholars, and their scholarship had only a limited impact on prevailing legal thinking[57].

The new legal system had different sources in addition to customary law (as opposed to written law) and existing trade regulations. The new regime brought about a new culture of lawmaking. The open exercise of highly concentrated state power as formulated by the Constitution of 1949 justified the intervention of party officials in the legislative process. The radical alteration of the entire regime in Hungary required swift and effective (state) administration. The sole function of public and professional debates was the legitimization of political decisions. Since the regime was to be built on a new elite that would, in theory, be comprised by those coming from the "lower classes." Where they existed, legal debates and discourses were orchestrated in newspapers rather than in professional journals or in monographs[58]. Later, the rivalry among various groups of legal elites became a new constellation. It was no longer connected to antagonisms among classical professional groups (judges, law clerks, attorneys), but to the position different specialists occupied in the power network of the party-state,

[56] 1080/1957. (X. 13.) Government decree on the government committees for codification.

[57] It is striking to see the difference in how conservative law professors managed to establish own schools in universities (ELTE), while their liberal counterparts did not. Examples are the Sólyom School, Mádl School, or the Harmathy School. In comparison, there is no Sárközy School or Sajó School *strictu sensu*.

[58] See, for example, Verebics, "A többi–néma csend."

which gave them more or less influence[59]. A formal role in the legislative process became a criterion of membership in the new legal elite. These employment opportunities provided special information as the source of special privileges, which was unknown to outsiders.

Thus, the traditional legal professionals were only involved in the legislative process through their representative bodies and not through their professional activities. Deprived of the ability to make law, judges simple became clerks and judicial administrators. Judges and courts represented a culturally hierarchical, traditional institution. They were generally not interested in the principles of law or in new legal thinking. Their careers depended on the statistics of their remanded cases. Therefore, it is very unlikely that a judge would decide or even argue against a decision by a superior court. The new laws and new ideas only made their lives uncomfortable.

As economic and financial crises endangered the regime and forced the country to open up to market requirements, "multipositioning" among the legal elites became commonplace once again. Toward the end of the socialist period but prior to the 1989 transition, bureaucrats enlisted experts, academics, and counselors from the private (business) sector in drafting new laws[60].

2.7. The rivalry of the legal elites in the post-socialist transition (1989–2017)

Historically, lawyers, especially those with foreign training (following the transition), tend to be more innovative in their legal application. These modernizing tendencies of lawyers are still apparent nowadays; academics often have private practices and lawyers have academic careers. These "multipositional" professors (and attorneys) are overrepresented in committees charged with drafting new laws.

The drafting of a new Civil Code took more than two decades, although the decision to create it was made fairly early in the 1990s[61]. A Codification Committee had already been established before the actual transition, and was operating in the Ministry of Justice in 1989. It was specifically organized to modernize the Civil Code of 1959[62]. The market legislation procedure, which was in full swing by that time, easily accommodated this objective. Led by academics, this com-

---

[59] It is intriguing how Tamás Sárközy explained the success of certain reforms towards the end of the socialist regime in the 1980s. For example, the Károly Grósz government was supported by János Kádár and other hardline socialist politicians. Therefore he could support new, "less socialist, more capitalist" institutions much easier than the reform economists in the party like Rezső Nyers. See Sárközy, *A szocializmus*.

[60] This was the business as usual when Tamás Sárközy served as Deputy Minister of Justice. See also Lengyel, *Fordulat és reform*.

[61] See Sárközy, *A szocializmus*, 214.

[62] Established by Tamás Sárközy. See Sárközy, *A szocializmus*, 216.

mittee remained in charge of the drafting process throughout the 1990s, though its activity slowed[63]. The next stage of the process began in 1998, when a new committee was organized by the incoming administration's Ministry of Justice[64]. There were eight academics, two lawyers, one prosecutor, two judges, and four bureaucrats and clerks in the drafting committee.

Taken together, academics and private sector lawyers were overrepresented in the new board of experts[65]. It seems that this drafting procedure finally reflected the tenets of Professorenrecht within the framework of the late-socialist regime.

Yet the drafting process was too slow. Although deliberations were indispensable for drawing up the new Civil Code, the rapid political transition, radical reconstruction of economic markets, new property relations, etc., required a swifter reaction. Consequently, dozens of amendments were made to the Civil Code of 1959 before the introduction of the new Civil Code. The drafters disagreed on fundamental issues: how broad should the scope of the Civil Code be?; should private law also cover corporate law?; should family law be included in the code?

Legal professionals supported different options (the Hungarian legal system's traditional solutions versus novel approaches based on either German or Anglo-Saxon traditions), but the main issues remained the same: whoever drafted the code would ultimately decide how legal studies would be taught in universities.

The basic conception of the new code was accessible to both the public and legal professionals on the website of the Ministry of Justice for a lengthy period of time (2000–2007). The entire process was based on an extensive professional debate, which has been accessible on-line[66].

In 2008, when everyone thought that the final draft of the code was finished, the new administration unexpectedly called for new initiatives to be incorporated into it[67]. On a practical level, this meant that the code had to be redrafted by the then-secretary of the Ministry of Justice[68]. Not surprisingly, this bill could not be fully reconciled with the 2007 drafting committee's proposals[69]. Major divergences

---

[63] Ibid. This was during the co-presidency of Attila Harmathy and Lajos Vékás. Both are professors at ELTE and members of the Hungarian Academy of Sciences.

[64] See 1050/1998. (IV. 24.) Government Decree, and 1061/1999. (V. 28.) Government Decree on the Civil Code. The leaders remained Attila Harmathy and Lajos Vékás. Pál Vastagh is a professor.

[65] Sources: 1050/1998. (IV. 24.) Government Decree, and 1061/1999. (V. 28.) Government Decree on the Civil Code.

[66] See the website www.ptk2013.hu.

[67] 1042/2008. (VI. 30.) Government decree repealing the government decree No. 1050/1998, and see the government decree No. 1049/2008. (VII. 18.) on the tasks related to the new Civil Code.

[68] Gábor Gadó was State Secretary at the Ministry of Justice and a lawyer and author of several professional articles. In an interview, he said he would not revise the bill again. His motivation was that the drafting committee was not ready to push through certain issues that were self-evident in other "developed" countries, such as the individual rights of disabled people, their representation in private life, or the rights of same-sex couples.

[69] See the Vékás committee, which expressed its discontent with the revised code.

concerned individual rights, especially those of disabled persons, and the recognition of same sex couples (family law).

Parliament began debating the bill and passed it in November 2009[70]. From that point on, the act became the subject of political games. By then, the overwhelming success of the conservative-nationalist opposition party (Fidesz) in the upcoming parliamentary elections seemed very likely. Thus, conservative, religious, and other lobbies played for time so that the new bill would not come into force. The president of the republic, a law professor himself who was long recognized for his opposition to the governing socialist party, vetoed the bill in November 2009, citing conceptual disagreements and procedural irregularities[71].

Notwithstanding the veto, the parliament passed an amended version of the bill in December 2009. Fidesz declared that if they won the election, the new Civil Code would not be put into effect, largely because of its discontent with the definition of marriage and same sex partnerships. In the meantime the parliament passed a supplementary bill that called for the gradual implementation of the new code to ensure it would be effective and manageable. In early 2010, Fidesz claimed the supplementary bill was unconstitutional and therefore null and void. The party referred the matter to the Constitutional Court, which upheld the position of the plaintiffs[72].

After ascending to power, the new Fidesz government established a new drafting committee, as promised[73]. The (partly) new draft of the Civil Code included entirely new sections as compared to the 2007 version[74]. This meant that the 2010 draft represented a fundamentally new conceptualization of legislative technique and—more importantly—philosophy of corporate law[75]. Although discussions had been ongoing since the post-communist transition (and even before), these sudden changes reflected the shifting power relations among academics, in addition to those among political parties.

In 2013, the new Civil Code Act was passed, and it entered into effect on March 15, 2014[76]. However, in December 2014, the Minister of Justice established a new drafting committee, charged with amending the new Civil Code of 2013, to be based in the ministry[77]. Bureaucrats significantly outnumbered academics in this committee, and those professors who were included held lower ranks—i.e., there

---

70 Act No. 2009. of CXX.

71 László Sólyom is a professor at ELTE University. He wrote an unexpectedly long letter of arguments touching upon professional rather than political issues.

72 The paradoxical outcome of which was that, due to legal prescriptions, there was a period of time in 2010 when two Civil Codes were in effect.

73 Under the presidency of Professor Lajos Vékás from ELTE University.

74 See the Vékás committee of 2007.

75 The main issue in this dispute was an old controversy, namely whether the Civil Code should also cover basic commercial law—i.e., the company law—or not. Professor Sárközy argued against, while Professor Vékás supported the inclusion.

76 Act of 2013. No. V. on the Civil Code.

77 László Tócsányi, a former judge, is Minister of Justice, lawyer, and university professor.

were fewer members of the Academy of Sciences on the committee[78]. The final draft of this committee modification of the 2013 Civil Code was passed by Parliament on June 13, 2016[79].

2.8. Contextual detour for possible comparisons

Undoubtedly, this case study of the civil code's drafting procedures requires a broader perspective. The following paragraphs provide some comparisons that clarify the procedural conditions of the drafting process of the post-transition Penal Code and Procedural Code.

The drafting of the Penal Code (2001–2012)[80] shows a shift towards the growing influence of the state administration, especially after 2010–2012. Thus, in 2001 there were twenty-two bureaucrats/clerks, twenty-four academics, twelve prosecutors, twelve judges, and fourteen lawyers, whereas in 2012 there were twenty-six bureaucrats/clerks, twenty academics, sixteen prosecutors, sixteen judges, and ten lawyers.

In the drafting of the Private Procedure Act (2010–2015)[81], bureaucratic leverage grew over time, marginalizing the academic fields. The drafting committees comprised of five bureaucrats/clerks, four academics, one prosecutor, four judges, and three lawyers.

2.9. Conclusion one: *Professorenrecht* revised in private law

Clearly, the German variety of Professorenrecht did not prevail in Hungary. Yet, academics still appear to have been one of the most influential elite groups among legal professionals involved in the process. Due to the expectation of objectivity by practitioners of legal sciences, academics—as opposed to other legal professionals— are the group most capable of concealing their own interests in proposals or recommendations, couching them in terms of efficiency or other socially recognized benefits. Nevertheless, there are other dimensions that alter the picture. The subject matter of regulations or laws makes a difference. In the case of the Civil Code, academics have been much more influential, whereas in the drafting of the Penal Code, this was not the case after 2010. Since the bureaucracy

---

78 These professors represent a younger generation that belonged to different (and some new) universities: Kinga Pázmándi is affiliated with the Budapest University of Technology and Economics; Zoltán Csehi is affiliated with Pázmány Péter Catholic University; Péter Miskolczi-Bodnár is affiliated with Károli Gáspár University of Reformed Churches in Hungary, and Attila Menyhárd is affiliated with ELTE.

79 See Act No. LXXVII of 2016, on the modification of the Civil Code of 2013.

80 *Büntetőjogi kodifikáció* 2001/1.

81 Government decree no. 1267/2013 (V. 17.).

and MPs traditionally have been less interested and willing to fully appreciate the complexity of economic issues, the context of competition, and market regulations, the leading role of academics and practicing lawyers is necessary, whereas in the case of the Penal Code, the Administrative Procedure Act, and other procedural codes, this is not as important. However, during the most recent parliamentary session, there were converging tendencies in this respect. The bureaucracy tends to impose its views in the realm of privacy and competition, which is clearly demonstrated in the case of the current Civil Code.

Especially after the Second World War, academics' influence has increased despite the fact that the bureaucracy has gained more leverage in the legislative process, and notwithstanding the growth of a specific profession charged with drafting legislation[82]. In Hungary there are no special courses for this activity and there is not much social and/or material prestige attached to it. Consequently, generally only newly-minted lawyers are recruited to be legal drafters. This is a recipe for very low administrative standards, which leaves a large amount of space for political and academic machinations.

The influence of academics remains relatively important despite the intervention of special interest groups, especially lobbyists, who act on behalf of pro-market forces and the welfare state. These groups are a reaction to administrative over-regulation and provide specific self-regulatory activity and soft laws[83]. The self-regulatory activities of practicing lawyers and their soft laws often have extended cross-border effects, since a company's investment decisions affect various regional stakeholders. Thus, academic leverage in the legislative process has gone global too, for example, in the various model laws of the Organization for Economic Cooperation and Development, the European Union (the Lando Commission, Hugh Beale), and the World Trade Organization. The leaders or the dominant elites in these working groups are almost exclusively professors. In short, Professorenrecht in Hungary may not hold the same meaning as in Germany, and it may not exert the same influence, but it does exist and plays a role in global legal harmonization.

[82] This influence became less relevant in the second and third Fidesz governments. See Varga, *A kodifikáció*, 379.

[83] Zumbansen, "What Lies Before," 4.

3. Constitutional law

3.1. Professorenrecht in constitutional law

The role or the notion of Professorenrecht appears to be very different in the development of constitutional law. If there was a working notion of *Professorenrecht*, it would most likely be in this field. Constitutional law is ideally based on pure categories in the Platonic sense, and on universal theories. It presumes, requires, and recognizes natural law or some sort of law related to basic human rights. If one defines constitutional law as the set of principles concerning the relationship between the state and the individual, then tenets of natural law must be accepted and there must be an acknowledgement that there are certain fundamental rights that protect the liberty of the individual from the government.

Nevertheless, without constitutional law there would still be a coherent legal system and a system of valid rules. Constitutional law simply contributes to the legitimacy and general acceptability of laws. Therefore if the constitution provides for the safeguard of private property, then seizures must be regulated (at least on the procedural level), and if equality before the law is guaranteed, then distinctions among different groups of people need to be specifically justified.

Constitutional law is a matter of more abstract thinking, the ideal terrain for academics. One might even say that it did not exist before the Enlightenment. Paradoxically enough, however, the articles and the entire operation of the Encyclopédistes might well be considered to be the first public and rather political discourse about the elements of a future constitution. By the same token, in Hungary the political debates of the so-called reform parliaments between 1825 and 1848 called for a public negotiation about the interpretation of the rights of persons as articulated in natural law and the constitutional principles of the country. When some of these concepts were integrated into the Laws of April 1848, political considerations far outweighed the legal ones proposed by academics[84].

However, traditional constitutional thinking appears to be different in Hungary. Although the constitution is not a matter of evolution, it is also not a purely theoretical construction. The Hungarian historical constitution is a kind of ancient pledge, an agreement of the nation and, in a certain sense, it still has a binding effect, having been revitalized in the new Basic Law of 2011[85]. With this in mind, one might have the impression that the contradictions evident in the practical influence of *Professorenrecht* in the sphere of private law are equally traceable in constitutional law. The two worlds, the traditional and the modernizing, clearly coexist within the same sociological setting.

---

[84] These so-called *"Laws of April"* might be considered an attempt to produce a written constitution.

[85] The meaning of the nation is not clear.

3.2. Continuous statehood, discontinuous constitutions

Act Number One of 2000 celebrated a millennium of Hungarian statehood. This emblematic piece of legislation—promoted especially by the traditionalist Hungarian Democratic Forum Party (MDF)—was drafted by the administration and submitted by the Minister of Justice (Ibolya Dávid, MDF). It demonstrated the deeply rooted fiction of the unbroken historical continuity of the country's constitutional traditions. Emblematic as it was, this statute also ordered that the crown (*Szent Korona* or the Holy Crown of St. István) and other royal coronation jewelry be placed in the House of the Parliament instead of the National Museum. This transfer was meant to reinvigorate the interpretation of the crown as the symbolic embodiment of the nation.

The preamble of the Basic Law of Hungary of 2011 affirms this position in its final sentences: "We are proud that our king St. Stephen founded our state on a solid foundation one thousand years ago and made our country a part of Christian Europe. [...] We honor the attainment of our historic Constitution and the Holy Crown, which embodies the continuous constitutional existence of the state of Hungary and the unity of the nation[86]." Yet, within the same credo, this alleged continuous existence is denied to certain eras of Hungarian history: "We do not acknowledge the communist constitution of 1949 because it was based on despotic power. Therefore we declare it to be null and void."[87] Clearly, by linking itself only to the 1919 revolution, the Constitution of 1949 declared itself to be a break in this "continuous historical constitutionalism."[88]

3.3. The birth of the first written constitution of 1949

The first written constitution of Hungary was conceptualized by the Hungarian Workers' Party (Magyar Dolgozók Pártja, MDP) as "the basic law of the peoples' democracy" in 1948. In the declaration of its program it stated that "the Party considers it necessary to create a basic law of the peoples' democracy in order to canonize the rights and duties of the citizens; the fundamental changes in public order, economy, and society; and the populist character of the republic" in the constitution.[89]

Since the allied party of the Hungarian Independent Peoples' Front, chaired by the communist leader Mátyás Rákosi, overwhelmingly won the elections of early May 1949, the drafting of this constitution faced no obstacles. Immediately after the inauguration, a drafting committee was established on May 27, 1949,

---

86 See the credo of the Basic Law of Hungary as amended.

87 Ibid.

88 See the Act No. XX. of 1949 on the Constitution of the People's Republic of Hungary. See also the preamble of the Act No. XX. of 1949 on the Constitution of the People's Republic of Hungary.

89 Beér, *Magyar alkotmányjog*, 111.

and was presided over by Rákosi himself, who was vice president of the Council of Ministers at the time.[90] The draft was approved by the government on August 5, 1949, and published for debate in popular gatherings organized in villages and factories across Hungary. The draft proposal was submitted to Parliament on August 10, and it was debated in committee on August 12. After negligible changes were made, the bill was passed on August 18, 1949, and published two days later.

It went into effect on the very same day, which was publicly celebrated as the "Constitution Day[91]." While neither the hastily generated constitutional text, nor the party's rhetoric or later commentary on the constitution denied that the ruling party's leaders were responsible for the draft, the regime was keen on demonstrating the widespread consent of the people[92]. Since academics were on the committee, the document could be said to bear the influence of Professorenrecht, though surely not in its original sense. The question is whether it is the ideological leverage of academics or that of politicians that defines the constitution. Certainly, the 1949 Constitution was a legal document, even if it was—admittedly—a translation of the 1936 Stalinist Soviet Constitution with the exception of the preamble and certain clauses.[93]

3.4. The birth of the constitution of the post-socialist transition in 1989

The drafting process of the 1989 Constitution had the exact opposite history as the Constitution of 1949. In addition to various domestic and international political and social factors, by the end of the 1980s, the desire to give genuine representative power back to Parliament served as the foundation of the Opposition Round Table (Ellenzéki Kerekasztal, EKA) on March 22, 1989, formed by the existing opponents of the regime and administered by the Independent Lawyers' Forum.

The EKA later created the so-called NEKA, the National Round Table (*Nemzeti Ellenzéki Kerekasztal*). The NEKA established a constitutional road map including

---

[90] The May 27, 1949, decision of the Council of Ministers. The members of this drafting committee also included Imre Szabó, a professor of law at ELTE, member of the Hungarian Academy of Sciences, and later the head of the Research Institute of the Academy, and Andor Berei, a professor of economics, president of the Planning Bureau in the 1950s, and a researcher at the Academy of Sciences.

[91] See Beér, *Magyar alkotmányjog*, 112.

[92] What is more, they were proud of it. See Beér, *Magyar alkotmányjog*.

[93] For example, Article 63 (2) declared that "the enemies of the working people and the mentally ill people are deprived of voting rights." Article 41 (1) stated that "the Courts of the Hungarian Peoples' Republic shall punish the enemies of the working peoples" Article 4 (2) provided that "working people shall gradually squeeze out the capitalists and shall build the socialist order of the economy."

how to modify and eventually redraft the existing Constitution of 1949.[94] The NEKA proceeded from the idea that new rules of governance and the rights and duties of the citizens would be drafted during the negotiations and then approved by the single-party Parliament, which would adopt the results of the political negotiations.

Thus, in 1989 the process took the opposite form of the 1949 process. Negotiations proceeded throughout the summer of 1989, and the public could follow them in the daily press or through other news channels. However, the news did not contain full transcripts of negotiations but provided only concise reports on the substance of the talks.[95]

The members of the NEKA were mostly academics and overwhelmingly lawyers or attorneys, especially those who represented the Independent Lawyers' Forum.[96] Conspicuously, actual law professors were less representative among the negotiators. Nevertheless, the entire founding procedure of the NEKA, and the essential discussions over the methods of the political negotiation process were held in the Criminal Law Department of ELTE's Faculty of Law. Not all of the representatives were democratically selected to carry out these negotiations, and no matter how favorable the environment was for constitutional reform later on in October 1989, the constitution that emerged from the NEKA negotiations was understood as a place holder[97]. The preliminary nature of this constitutional change was declared in its short preamble, and from a legal-administrative standpoint, the 1989 Constitution was merely an amendment to the Constitution of 1949. Later on, as the "changes" decreased in popularity, these factors led to a conti nuous process of constitutional revision.

---

[94] On June 10, 1989, the NEKA began negotiations with the ruling Socialist Party (MSZMP). The opposition contained the Bajcsy-Zsilinszky Society and the representatives of the parties that would later to become the MDF, FKGP, MSZDP, SZDSZ, MSZP, FIDESZ, and the trade unions.

[95] Participation in the NEKA: six non-law professors, twenty-five lawyers, five representatives of the Communist Party, and eleven other professionals.

[96] There were four law professors and nineteen practicing lawyers in the NEKA. These numbers are based on Bozóki, *"Szemérmes alkotmányozás,"* 216. The participants of the first meeting were Károly Vigh, László Kövér, Viktor Orbán, Pál György Bártfay, Imre Kónya, György Sándorfi, Imre Boross, András Gergely, György Szabad, Csaba Varga, Bálint Magyar, László Bruszt, László Vitézy, and T. Mihály Révész. However, many others joined the negotiations, including László Sólyom, János Kis, Péter Tölgyessy, Béla Pokol, etc. The majority of these negotiators were lawyers and academics. Different meetings included different participants.

[97] Körösényi, Tóth, and Török, *A magyar politikai rendszer*; and especially Jakab, "A magyar alkotmányjog-tudomány." See Act No. XXXI. of 1989 on the Amendment of the Constitution (of Act No. XX. of 1949) regarding the temporary status of the constitution.

3.5. The birth of the Basic Law of 2011

The Basic Law of 2011 was drafted on the private iPad of a member of Fidesz.[98] This hastily written document was based on the previous constitution; some parts of it are an exact "copy and paste." Nevertheless, there has never been a written constitution that was as hotly debated in academic circles as this one. There were already many drafts of a new constitution circulating in the 1990s, because the 1989 Constitution's legitimacy had always been questioned.[99] It is, therefore, interesting that after so many debates and so much preparation, the Basic Law did not actually reflect any of the concerns, fears, or proposals raised during the previous two decades.[100]

Having said that, the question of *Professorenrecht* is disguised, but present. Although the Orbán regime might be described as a legalistic or legalizing regime, this identity is mirrored neither in the strengthening of *Professorenrecht*, nor in the legislation proposed by the administration or Fidesz's legislation proposals. The influence of political will is comparable to that which accompanied the drafting of the 1949 Constitution.

3.6. Conclusion two: Professorenrecht revised in constitutional law

One might have the impression that the notion of Professorenrecht was still valid in the field of constitutional law in a confusing and limited way. Perhaps not surprisingly, political leverage remains more influential in these cases than in the creation of civil or private law. In principle, a constitution drafted by academics rather than politicians, and thus in a less transparent and more undemocratic manner similar to the Weimar Constitution, is not inherently problematic. This method is far better than a written constitution drafted by a victorious general like the Japanese constitution, despite its effectiveness and durability. Yet, it is important to consider that even if many constitutional drafting processes are characterized by a lack of democratic control or legitimacy, the people involved do not universally try to convince the citizenry that the opposite is true. One could say that the litmus test of a constitutional democratic regime is whether the ruling elite feels it is necessary to demonstrate the consent of an overwhelming majority of people in favor of a newly drafted constitution or whether this same elite can handle the fact that the constitution is merely a legal-theoretical piece of work.

---

98 See "iPaden írja az alkotmányt." This member of the Fidesz Party, József Szájer, is also member of the European Parliament, and was on an academic track at the beginning of his career.

99 See, for example, Halmai, "Egy új alkotmánymodell felé"; Bragyova, *Az új alkotmány*; Ádám et al., "Mire való az alkotmányozás?"

100 For a brief summary, see Jakab, "*A magyar alkotmányjog-tudomány*," 186–88.

REFERENCES

1. "A Ptk. Tervezetének vitája az Állam- és Jogtudományi Intézetben" [Debate on the draft proposal of the Civil Code, held in the Institute of State- and Legal Sciences]. Jogtudományi Közlöny 13, nos. 3–4 (1958): 129–32.
2. Ádám, Antal, Géza Kilényi, András Sajó, Péter Schmidt, László Perecz, and Vilmos Sós. "Mire való az alkotmányozás?" [What is the drafting of the constitution good for?]. Világosság 35, no. 12 (1994): 5–27.
3. Asztalos, László. "A magyar burzsoá magánjog rövid története" [Concise history of the Hungarian bourgeois private law]. In Polgári jogi tanulmányok [Civil law studies], 5–302. Budapest: ELTE ÁJK Polgári jogi tanszék, 1970.
4. Beér, János, ed. Magyar alkotmányjog [Hungarian constitutional law]. Budapest: Tankönykiadó, 1951.
5. Bilét, Menyhért. "A redintegrációról" [On redintegration]. Jogtudományi Közlöny, March 1924.
6. Bozóki, András. "Szemérmes alkotmányozás. Rendszerváltás és jogállami forradalom 1989-ben" [The chaste drafting of the constitution: The changes and the rule of law revolution in 1989]. In Alkotmányozás Magyarországon és máshol [Drafting of the constitution in Hungary and elsewhere], edited by András Jakab and András Körösényi, 202–39. Budapest: MTA TK PTI—Új Mandátum, 2012.
7. Bragyova, András. Az új alkotmány egy koncepciója [A concept of the new constitution]. Budapest: Közgazdasági és Jogi Könyvkiadó—MTA Állam- és Jogtudományi Intézet, 1995.
8. Cserne, Péter, and György Gajduschek. "Jogalkotási javaslatok megfogalmazása a jogtudományban" [Proposals for legislation in legal scholarship]. In A jog tudománya.
9. [Jurisprudence], edited by András Jakab and Attila Menyhárd, 79–100. Budapest: HVG-Orac, 2015.
10. Dezső, Márta, Klára Fürész, István Kukorelli, Imre Papp, János Sári, Bernadette Somody, Péter Szegvári, Imre Takács. Alkotmánytan [Constitutional studies]. Vol. 1. Budapest: Osiris Kiadó, 2007.
11. Georch, Illés Ettre-Karchai. Honnyi törvény [Domestic laws]. Vols. 1–2. Pozsony: Belnay György Aloys, 1804–1806.
12. Halmai, Gábor, ed. Egy új alkotmánymodell felé [Towards a new constitutional model]. Budapest: Társadalomtudoményi Társaság, 1991.
13. Hamza, Gábor. "Vécsey Tamás és a jogi szemináriumok" [Tamás Vécsey and the law seminars]. Jogtörténeti Szemle. Special issue (2005): 12–21.
14. Hesselink, Martijn W. The New European Private Law: Essays on the Future of Private Law in Europe. The Hague: Kluewer Law International, 2002.
15. Horváth, Pál. "Tudós elmék és eredmények a hazai modern jogi tudományosság kifejlődésében" [Scientific minds and results in the development of the Hungarian legal studies]. Jogtörténeti Szemle. Special Issue (2005): 21–26.
16. Ip, Eric C. "Globalization and the Future of the Law of the Sovereign State." International Journal of Constitutional Law 8, no. 3 (2010): 636–55.
17. Jakab, András. "A magyar alkotmányjog-tudomány története és jelenlegi helyzete" [The past and current situation of the Hungarian constitutional law studies]. In

A jog tudománya, edited by András Jakab and Attila Menyhárd, 159–92. Budapest, HVG-Orac, 2015.

18. Körösényi, András, Csaba Tóth, and Gábor Török. A magyar politikai rendszer [The Hungarian political system]. Budapest: Osiris Kiadó, 2003.
19. Lengyel, László, ed. Fordulat és reform [Turnaround and reform]. Budapest: Pénzügykutató, 1986.
20. Menyhárd, Attila. "A polgári jog tudománya Magyarországon" [The jurisprudence of civil law in Hungary]. In A jog tudománya, edited by András Jakab and Attila Menyhárd, 218–60. Budapest: HVG-ORAC, 2015.
21. Menyhárd, Attila, and András Jakub, eds. A jog tudománya [Jurisprudence]. Budapest, HVG-Orac, 2015.
22. Mezey, Barna. "Jogalkotás a 16–19. századi Magyarországon" [Legislation in Hungary in the 16th–19th centuries]. Rubicon, nos. 1–2 (2012): 76–81.
23. —. "A jogászképzés változásai" [Changes in the legal education]. Jogtörténeti Szemle. Special issue (2005): 1–3.
24. —. "Wlassics Gyula, a büntetőjog és a bűnvádi perjog professzora" [Gyula Wlassics, the professor of criminal law and criminal procedure law]. In Wlassics Gyula és kora 1852–1937 [Gyula Wlassics and his time, 1852–1937], edited by Imre Kapiller, 60–78. Zalaegerszeg: Millecentenáriumi Közalapítvány, 2002.
25. Peschka, Vilmos. "Thibaut és Savigny vitája" [The debate of Thibaut and Savigny]. Állam- és Jogtudomány, no. 3 (1974): 353–81.
26. Ráth, György. Az Országbírói értekezlet a törvénykezés tárgyában [The general meeting of the chief judge]. Pest: Landerer és Heckenast, 1861.
27. Sajó, András. Kritikai értekezés a jogtudományról [Critical analysis of jurisprudence]. Budapest: Akadémiai Kiadó, 1983.
28. Sárközy, Tamás. "A jog szerepe a gazdaságban" [The role of the law in the economy]. Magyar Tudomány, no. 5 (2011): 535–40.
29. —. A szocializmus, a rendszerváltás és az új kapitalizmus gazdasági civiljoga 1945–2005 [The civil law of socialism, the regime transition, and the new capitalism, 1945–2005]. Budapest, HVG-Orac, 2007.
30. Schepel, Harm. "Professorenrecht? The Field of European Private Law." In In Lawyers' Circles: Lawyers and European Legal Integration, edited by Harm Schepel and Alex Jettinghoff, 115–24. The Hague: Elsevier Reed, 2004.
31. Somogyvári, István. "Magyar alkotmányozás 1988–2008" [Hungarian drafting of the constitution, 1988–2008]. Politikaiévkönyv.hu, 1995. http://www.politikaievkonyv. hu/online/mp20/1-02_somogyvari.html.
32. Szűcs, Jenő. Nemzet és történelem [Nation and history]. Budapest: Gondolat Kiadó, 1984.
33. Szuromi, Szabolcs. "A középkori egyetemek létrejöttének és az egyetemi oktatás megszületésének sajátosságai" [Special characteristics of the emergence of medieval universities and university education]. Jogtörténeti Szemle. Special Issue (2005): 3–7.
34. Varga, Csaba. A kodifikáció mint társadalmi-történelmi jelenség [Codification as a socio-historical phenomenon]. Budapest: Akadémiai Kiadó, 1979.
35. Verebics, János. "'A többi—néma csend.' A száz éve született Világhy Miklós pályaképe" ["The rest is silence": Curriculum Vitae of Miklós Világhy, born 100

years ago]. In Emlékülés Világhy Miklós születésének 100. évfordulója alkalmából [Conference in memoriam of Miklós Világhy on the hundredth anniversary of his birthday]. Budapest: Magyar Jogászegyleti Értekezések, 2017.

36. Zumbansen, Peer C. "What Lies Before, Behind, and Beneath a Case? Five Minutes on Transnational Lawyering and the Consequences for Legal Education." Research paper no. 62/2013, Osgoode Hall Law School of York University, Comparative Research in Law and Political Economy.

www.ingramcontent.com/pod-product-compliance
Lightning Source LLC
Chambersburg PA
CBHW071352230926
51846CB00002B/520